What They Didn't Teach You in **Italian** Class

Slang phrases for the café, club, bar, bedroom, game and more

Gabrielle Euvino

ULYSSES PRESS

Published by:
Ulysses Press
P.O. Box 3440
Berkeley, CA 94703
www.ulyssespress.com

ISBN: 978-1-64604-396-5 (paperback)
ISBN: 978-1-61243-678-4 (hardback)
Library of Congress Control Number: 2016957697

Printed in the United States
10 9 8 7 6 5 4 3 2 1

Managing editor: Claire Chun
Editors: Shayna Keyles, Alice Riegert
English proofreader: Lauren Harrison
Italian proofreader: Lorenza Cerbini
Design and illustrations: what!design @ whatweb.com
Production: Yesenia Garcia-Lopez

Mille grazie to my dear *amici, studenti,* and *famiglia* for making me smile through life's travails.

Contents

Using This Book 7

Chapter 1 Meet & Greet 13

Chapter 2 Friends & Flirting 32

Chapter 3 Booze, Bars, & Clubs 55

Chapter 4 Sexy Body, Ugly Body 68

Chapter 5 Nice & Naughty 85

Chapter 6 Smack Talk 109

Chapter 7 Pop Culture, Fashion, & Technology 132

Chapter 8 Sports & Games 154

Chapter 9 Dining & Desserts 166

Acknowledgments 181

About the Author 183

Un linguaggio diverso è una diversa visione della vita.
A different language is a different vision of life.

—Federico Fellini

Il più bel fiore ne coglie.
She picks the fairest flower.

—Petrarch

Using This Book

You may remember struggling to stay awake in your eighth period high school *classe di italiano*. All those verb drills and conjugations, the teacher droning on and on, and you doodling along the margins of your secondhand textbook. You skipped class, failed your tests, and thought the period would never end. Who cares about *la grammatica, i verbi*, and *il vocabolario*, anyway?

Now, imagine what your *esperienza* could have been: Your textbook is a copy of *What They Didn't Teach You in Italian Class*. The teacher starts waving his or her arms and cursing, inciting the class to "*ripetete*!" Together, you chant "*Merda!...Figlio di puttana... porca miseria...*" ("Shit!...Son of a bitch...miserable swine..."). It's doubtful you would have ever missed a day of school again.

Italians are some of the most *generosi, originali*, and gifted *scrittori* (writers), *artisti, scienziati*, musicians, mathematicians, thinkers, *filosofi* (philosophers), and *maestri* (teachers) that *il mondo* has ever known. Italians invented half the stuff you take for granted. They gave the world banks, batteries, and one of the earliest dictionaries; they created espresso machines, *autostrade* (highways) and the first internal combustion engine; they invented liposuction, *profumi* (perfumes), pianos, and *pistole* (pistols). They gave us artificial insemination, cloning, and condoms. *Grazie* to the Italians, you can listen to talk radio and *telefonare* (telephone) your BFF.

That same *creatività* comes through in their language. And, just like their particular strengths are demonstrated by their many achievements, when life happens, the Italians have a way with words that is unsurpassed. In linguistic terms, Italian was called a vulgar language for the simple reason that it was spoken by the common folk. Writers like Boccaccio, Dante, Machiavelli, and Shakespeare all drew inspiration from that same "vulgar" vocabulary. And while you shouldn't expect to be quoting Dante here, by the time you're done reading, you'll certainly be able to describe *che merdaio* (what a shithole) hell can be.

What They Didn't Teach You in Italian Class is designed to offer you an understanding of the Italian *cultura e lingua* used behind closed doors, outside school, and in the office. It's the language whispered among lovers, screamed among haters and hell-raisers, and includes all the sleaze you could ever please. I've tried to offer the reader as much of the Italian *lingua* he or she might hear or have heard along the way that would be inappropriate to teach in most classroom settings. If you're easily offended, I suggest you put the book down right now. Misuse of this book could result in the loss of *amici* (friends), *amanti* (lovers), and your sweet *culo* (ass). Now, let's get started! *Buon divertimento!*

Italian pronunciation
La pronuncia italiana

Per fortuna, unlike English, Italian is a very reasonable language when it comes to figuring out the pronunciation. The first thing you should do is add a vowel to the end of every word. No *problema!* Just fake it till you make it!

Also in your favor is the fact that Italian and English share a lot of cognates; these are words that look and sound like each other (*banana, stupido, problema*, etc.) but are from different languages (like banana, stupid, problem, etc.). You'll see quite a few of them throughout the book.

Italian is a phonetically based language. Keep this basic rule in mind: What you see, you say. The Italian alphabet is just like the English alphabet, minus the letters "j," "k," "w," "x," and "y" (although they are used with foreign words and names). For example, both English and Italian possess the same hard "k" sound, but utilize different letters to get there. Think of Chianti wine, and you begin to get it.

The vowels are pronounced:

> **A** sounds like "ah," as in *amore* (ah-MOH-reh), meaning "love"
>
> **E** sounds like "eh," as in *sesso* (ses-soh), meaning "sex"
>
> **I** sounds like "ee," as in *imbecille* (eem-beh-CHEEL-leh), meaning "imbecile"
>
> **O** sounds like "oh," as in *zitto* (ZEET-toh), meaning "Shut up!"
>
> **U** sounds like "oo," as in *nudo* (NOO-doh), meaning "nude"

For practice, try utilizing all five vowels at the same time with the word *aiuole* (flowerbeds), pronounced ay-YOO-wah-leh.

There are no silent letters in Italian, except any word that begins with "h," such as "hotel" (pronounced oh-tel).

Certain letter combinations differ from English. Instead of remembering rules, use these examples:

> **ch** is pronounced like "k," as in *chiacchierare* (kyah-kyeh-RAH-reh) (to gossip)
>
> **ci** is like the "ch" sound in English, as in *ciao*
>
> **ce** also sounds like "ch," as in *centro* (pronounced CHEN-troh)
>
> **ge** and **gi** are pronounced like a "j," as in *gelato* ("ice cream") and *Gino*
>
> **gh** is pronounced like it's used in English in words like ghetto (an Italian word)

gn sounds like "ni" like the word "companion," as in *bagno* (pronounced *BAHN-yoh*) and *gnocchi* (pronounced NYOHK-kee)

oi is pronounced "oy," as in *troia* (pronounced TROY-ah)

r is very lightly trilled

rr should sound like the purr of a pussycat—just don't overdo it

s sounds like the "s" in "sun," as in sole (pronounced *SOH-leh*) when it begins a word, but if it's inside a word it sounds more like a "z," as in casa (pronounced KAH-zah)

ss when pronounced inside a word is like the word "sassy"

sc plus the vowels "a," "o," and "u" is pronounced with a hard "k" sound (*scandalo, scopare, scusa*)

sc plus the vowels "e" and "i" is pronounced with a soft "sh" sound like *pesce* (pronounced PEH-sheh), and *sci* (pronounced like "she")

zz is easily remembered by the word "pizza" and pronounced tz

Take your double consonants seriously: always linger on them a little longer. *Pene* with one "n" means "penis"...while the word *penne* refers to pasta (it's also the word for "pens").

Don't stress out about where to put the emphasis in Italian. For words of two syllables, you should lightly emphasize the first syllable. For example, the word *merda* (shit) would be pronounced *MER-dah*. With longer words, the stress is generally placed on the second-to-last syllable; the verb *incazzare* (to piss off) is pronounced *een-katz-ZAH-reh*. Any word ending in an accent is stressed on the last syllable, such as *città* (city), pronounced *cheet-TAH*.

Italian grammar

La grammatica italiana

I know, grammar schmammar. But it doesn't hurt to have quick primer on what's what. You learned all this once, but you were probably too bored, pent up, and fixated on the cute guy or girl in the next desk to pay *attenzione*. So here it is again, even if not much has changed since middle school.

Every noun has a gender, either masculine or feminine. Most Italian nouns require the use of the definite article. The singular articles are *il*, which is used in front of most masculine nouns, like *il figo* (the hottie); *la*, which is used in front of most feminine nouns, like *la fanciulla* (the chick); l', used in front of any noun that begins with a vowel, like *l'ignorante* (the ignoramus); and *lo*, used in front of a masculine noun that begins with a "z" or with an "s" plus a consonant, like *lo scemo* (the fool). The plural definite articles are *i*, *gli*, and *le*.

TO BE OR NOT TO BE: THE VERB *ESSERE*

In order to judge people, you're going to want to have a basic understanding of the verb *essere* (to be). Calling someone a "dumbass" will be a lot more effective if you can avoid saying, "You is a dumbass."

I am	*io sono*
you are	*tu sei*
you are (formal)	*Lei è* (capitalization indicates formality, in this case)
he is	*lui è*
she is	*lei è*
we are	*noi siamo*
you are (plural)	*voi siete* (in other words, "you guys")
they are	*loro sono*

Adjectives must agree with the nouns they modify. Whenever you see words like *bello/a* (beautiful) or *brutto/a* (ugly), the "/a" is there to remind you that you need to change your adjective if the subject is feminine. Foreign words like "sexy" remain the same whether you're speaking about a man or a woman.

My dog is **beautiful** and nice.
*Il mio cane è **bello** e simpatico.*

My girlfriend is **beautiful** and funny.
*La mia ragazza è **bella** e buffa.*

Possessives follow the same rules as adjectives and always reflect the gender and number of the thing(s) being possessed, like when you say *Mamma mia.*

DIMINUITIVES AND SUPERLATIVES

Italian allows speakers to modify nouns and adjectives by using diminutives and superlatives. Here are some useful adapters.

-accio typically gives a negative connotation to something

un tipo, un tipaccio (a dude, a jerkoff)

-etto makes things more familiar and cuter

il culo, il culetto (the ass, the cute ass)

-ino makes nouns and adjectives smaller or less than

il gatto piccolo (the small cat)

il gattino piccolino (the tiny cat)

-issimo exaggerates adjectives

bello/a, bellissimo/a (beautiful, gorgeous)

-one makes things bigger

il cazzo, il cazzone (the dick, the big dick)

CHAPTER 1

Meet & Greet

Incontrare & Conoscere

Before you can get *veramente* (truly) down and dirty in Italy, you're going to need to warm up a little. Italian small talk is the equivalent of linguistic foreplay, the *antipasto*, or the meal before the meal. Stretch your *lingua* (tongue) with these common Italian greetings and icebreakers.

Breakin' the ice

Rompere il ghiaccio

Ciao has become a popular way of greeting friends all over the world. Italians are notorious for their flatteries. No one ever minds if you add *bello* or *bella* after this little word.

Hi/bye!
Ciao!

Hi, handsome/beautiful!
Ciao bello/a!

Hi, gorgeous!
Ciao bellissimo/a!

Hiya!
Salve!

Whatcha' up to?
Cosa fai?

How's it goin'?
Come va?

Hey, boss!
Ciao, capo!

Good morning!
Buon giorno!
This is used to mean both "good morning" and "good day."

Good evening!
Buona sera!
This is used in the afternoon and evening when greeting people, as well as to say "goodbye."

It's a beautiful day!/evening!
Bella giornata!/serata!

Good night!
Buona notte!

Goodbye!
Saluti!

There are two ways of asking someone their name, politely or familiarly:

What's your name? (polite)
Come si chiama?

What do you go by? (familiar)
Come ti chiami?

Do you speak English? (polite)
Parla l'inglese?

Do you speak English? (familiar)
Parli l'inglese?

Dialogue
Dialogo

How are ya?
Come stai?

What's up?
Che c'è?

What's the word?
Tutto bene?
Literally, "Everything good?"

What's good?
Cosa c'è di bello?

What's there to talk about?
Che si dice?

What's new?
Cosa c'è di nuovo?

Any news?
Novità?

How's it goin'?
Come va?

> It's goin' well.
> *Va bene.*
>
> Can't complain.
> *Non mi lamento.*
>
> Eh...
> *Beh...*
>
> Everything's cool.
> *Tutto a posto.*
> Literally, "everything in place."

Epic!
Fico!
This word is used to describe a lot of things, and you'll see different meanings associated with it throughout the book.

Fantastic!
Fantastico!

Getting by.
Mi arrangio.

Good!
Bene!

You work with what you've got.
Si arrangia con quello che c'è.
From the verb *arrangiarsi* (to deal with things). *L'arte di arrangiarsi* describes "the art of figuring shit out."

Good enough!
Benone!

Great!
Benissimo!

Hanging in there.
Me la cavo.
From the verb *cavarsela* (to manage).

Not bad.
Mica male.

Shitty.
Di merda.

So-so.
Così-così.

Whatever...
Insomma...

How's it hanging?
Che aria tira?

It's better if you don't ask.
Meglio che non me lo chiedi.

What do you care?
Che te ne importa?

See you soon!
A presto!

If you've ever spent *le feste* (the holidays) with an Italian *famiglia*, you know that Italian goodbyes can take as long as the visit itself.

Take care!
Prenditi cura!

Be well!
Stammi bene!

See you!
Ci vediamo!

TITLES
TITOLI

Italians address strangers the way we used to in the U.S., back in the day when Americans were polite, using Mr. (*Signore*) or Mrs./ Ms. (*Signora*) or Miss (*Signorina*). Always err on the side of excessive formality, especially when meeting *i genitori* (the parents) of your new Italian friend.

It's a pleasure to meet you, Mr. Ciaula.
***E' un piacere** conoscerLa, Signore Ciaula.*
The pronoun is capitalized to indicate the formal "you."

It's a pleasure to make your **acquaintance**, Mrs. Troia.
*E' un piacere fare la Sua **conoscenza**, Signora Troia.*

Excuse me, miss, but have we met?
***Mi scusi,** signorina, ma ci siamo già conosciuti?*

Maybe I'll catch you in the piazza later on?
Ci troviamo piùtardi in piazza ***magari****?*

Good night!
Buona notte!

Later!
A più tardi!

I gotta bounce.
Devo andarmene.

See ya tomorrow.
A domani.

I can't wait!
Non vedo l'ora!
Literally, "I don't see the hour," meaning time can't pass fast enough.

Goodbye!
Arrivederci!

Call me!
Chiamami!

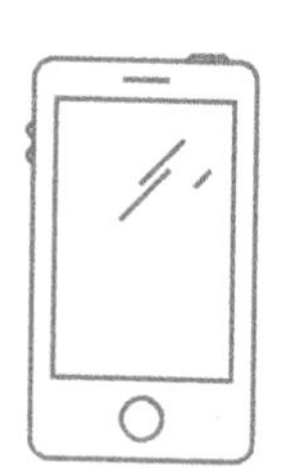

Text me!
Mandami un SMS!
Pronounced "ESS-ay EM-ay ESS-ay."

I'm outta here.
Me ne vado.

Peace!
Pace!

How's life treating you?
Come ti va la vita?

One of the coolest things about an Italian city is *la piazza*, essentially the town square. It's where Italians go to ogle one another, to show off their good looks, and to meet up before going out. Look for a marble cherub pissing into a *fontana* or some bronze *statua* of a dead poet or soldier, and you'll know you're there.

Trying to find your way around the maze of *strade* (roads) in an Italian town or city can be a total nightmare. If you don't know how to find a *piazza*, follow the bull's-eye symbol toward *centro* ("center," or downtown) and you'll find one for sure.

Hey!
Ehi!

Look who's coming!
***Guarda** chi c'è!*

Damn! How long has it been?
***Accidenti!** Da quanto tempo non ti vedo?*

How's your wifey/hubby?
***Come** sta la tua mogliettina/il tuo maritino?*

Long time **no see**!
***Non ci vediamo** da tanto tempo!*

It's good to see you.
Sono felice di vederti.

What a **pleasure** to see you!
*Che **piacere** vederti!*

What've you been up to?
Che hai combinato?

Where've you been?
***Dove** sei stato/a?*

Please, thank you, and sorry
Per favore, grazie, e mi dispiace

Please!
Per favore!

Pleez!
Per piacere!

Thanks./Thanks a million.
Grazie./Mille grazie.

Thanks a lot.
Tante grazie.

Thanks for fuckin' nothing.
Grazie al cazzo!

Don't mention it.
Non c'è di che.

It's nothing.
Non fa niente.

You're welcome.
Prego.
Like *ciao, prego* is another multipurpose word that can mean a lot more than "you're welcome." It also means "no prob," "after you," "make yourself comfortable," and "cool." When Italians say *Ti prego!*, they're really saying "I'm beggin' ya!" or "You gotta do me this favor!"

Excuse me.
Mi scusi.

Capeesh?
Hai capito?

I get it.
Ho capito.

I'm with ya.
Ti capisco.
Literally, "I understand."

I'm following.
Ti seguo.

Sorry.
Mi dispiace.

My bad!
Mea culpa!

Ooops!
Ops!

My fault!
Colpa mia!

It's totally **my fault**!
*È tutta **colpa mia**!*

I messed up big time!
Ho cannato alla grande.

What a **screw-up**!
*Che **puttanata**!*
From the word *puttana* (whore).

Forgive me, man.
***Scusami**, amico.*

My sincere **apologies**.
*Chiedo **scusa**.*

Let's talk weather
Parliamo del tempo

Why do Italians talk about *il tempo* (the weather)? Because even if you have absolutely nothing else in common, you're both alive and breathing, standing underneath the same *cielo* (sky). It's a start. There's nothing like talking about the shitty *tempo* to break an awkward *silenzio*.

What's the weather like?
Che tempo fa?

It's....
È....

a nice day
una bella giornata

nice out
bello

bleak
brutto

shitty out today
una merda oggi

a really **shitty** day
proprio una giornata ***di merda***

It's cold.
Fa freddo.

It's friggin' **cold**.
Fa un ***freddo*** *cane.*
Literally, "it's dog cold."

It's **hot** as hell.
Fa un ***caldo*** *infernale.*

It's a fuckin' oven.
C'è un caldo bestiale.
Literally, "a beastly heat."

The weather **sucks**.
Il tempo fa ***schifo***.

It's not that bad.
Non è poi così brutto.

What's up with the fucking **rain** today?
Ma che cazzo ***piove*** *oggi?*

Do I know you?
Ci conosciamo?

It may seem like the most obvious pickup line in the book, but it works like a charm. The next time you want to pick up an Italian girl, pretend like you're long-lost *amici*.

You're leaving already? Can I **come with you**?
*Vai già via? Posso **accompagnarti**?*

Can I **give you a hand**?
*Posso **darti una mano**?*

Can I **offer you a drink**?
*Posso **offrirti qualcosa da bere**?*

Can you **light me up**?
*Hai d'**accendere**?*

Are you from around **here**?
*Sei di **qua**?*

Wanna **go out** sometime?
*Ti va di **uscire** insieme qualche volta?*

Can I get your...?
***Posso** avere il tuo...?*

> **number**
> *numero di telefono*
>
> **address**
> *indirizzo*

I wanna see you **this evening**.
*Voglio vederti **stasera**.*

Who are you, where did you come from, and where are you going?
***Chi sei**, da dove vieni, e dove vai?*

It feels like I've known you **forever**.
*Mi sento di conoscerti da **sempre**.*

You look just like the first girl I ever fell in love with.
Assomigli tanto *alla prima ragazza di cui mi sono innamorato.*

Do you want to go out or should I just **go fuck myself**?
*Vuoi uscire o vado a **farmi fottere**?*

And for ladies who are sick of hearing the same cliché B.S....

Sorry, I'm **engaged**.
*Mi dispiace, sono **fidanzata**.*

Don't take it personally; I'm a **lesbian**.
*Non te la prendere; sono **lesbica**.*

I don't see you that way, but I hope we can stay **friends**.
*Non ti vedo in quella maniera, ma spero di rimanere **amici**.* (Ouch!)

You can't imagine how much I value you and your **friendship**.
*Tu non immagini quanto tengo a te e alla tua **amicizia**.*

You're kidding, right?
***Scherzi**, vero?*

I'm not that **desperate**!
*Non sono mica così **disperata**!*

What **planet** are you from?
*Ma da che **pianeta** vieni?*

Good luck!
Buona fortuna!

During Roman times, bloodthirsty spectators chanted in Latin *quasso crusis* (break a leg) to wish the gladiators good luck. The expression actually refers to the bending of one's leg, hopefully to pick up the money that audiences used to pelt their favorite players with, or later, the flowers that would be thrown onto the stage.

What fuckin' luck!
Che culo!
Literally, "what ass."

You're a lucky son of a bitch!
Che culo che hai!
Literally, "what an ass you have!"

Kick ass!
In culo alla balena!
Literally, "up the ass of the whale!" Here, the appropriate response would be: *Speriamo che non caghi!* ("Here's hoping he doesn't shit!")

What shit luck!
Che sfiga!

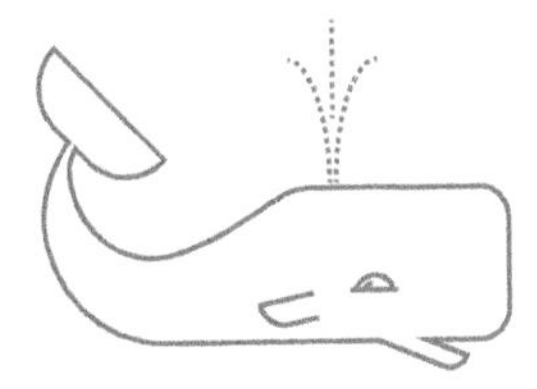

Best of luck!
In bocca al lupo!
Literally, "in the mouth of the wolf."

You're kidding!
Ma stai scherzando!

There are a lot of words and exclamations used to express that we're *totally* with someone when they're speaking. In English, we say things like "No way!" and "I hear you." Believe me, if you toss out some of these *espressioni*, you'll have everyone convinced that you understand way more than you actually do.

Are you kidding?
Scherzi?

I don't believe it.
Non ci credo.

For real?
Davvero?

Seriously?
Sul serio?

Come on!
Dai!

Yeah, right!
Ma va!

Exactly.
Appunto.

Check it out.
Che roba.
Literally, "what stuff."

For sure.
Di sicuro.

Get outta here!
Sparisci!

I agree.
D'accordo.

I understand.
Capisco.

No way!
Non me lo dire...ma va!

Totally.
Assolutamente.

Without a **doubt.**
*Senza **dubbio.***

You know it.
***Sai** com'è.*

Crazy!
Pazzesco!

Damn!
Accidenti!

Horrible!
Orribile!

Scandalous!
Scandaloso!

Seductive!
Seducente!

You're crazy!
Sei pazzo/a!

You're nuts!
Sei matto/a!

You're out of your **mind.**
Sei fuori ***testa.***

How come?
Come mai?

WOW!
WOW!

Italians are known for their *passione* and enthusiasm. Any of the following are used to say "Wow!"

Wow!
Ammappa!
Used mostly in central Italy.

Hot damn!
Ammazza!
Used throughout Italy to express incredulity.

Man! Holy shit!
Caspita!

Whoa!
Mamma mia!
Literally, "my mother."

Incredible!
Incredibile!

Fuck yeah!
Cazzo!
Literally means "dick" and is on the extreme of the vulgar scale... which doesn't stop millions of Italians from using it every day.

Fucking A!
Cacchio!
The word also refers to a weiner (or a cactus).

Win!
Cavolo!
A euphemism for *cazzo*, which literally translates to "cabbage."

Who knows?
Chissà?

You're messing with me.
Mi prendi in giro.
Literally, "you're taking me for a spin."

I swear.
Ti giuro.

Yep.
È già.
È già means "already," but is used when someone states the obvious.

If only!
Magari!
Italians use this to express something desirable that's probably never gonna happen, like "Yeah, when pigs fly!"

What a mess
Che pasticcio

Just because Italians live in a country that often looks like a scene out of a *favola* (fairy tale) doesn't mean they're always living one. Even with one of the most gorgeous populations on the planet combined with the most delish *piatti* (dishes) your palate could ever hope for, life happens. Traffic jams, flat tires, strikes, fires, heartbreaks, deaths, illness, mullets...not everything is a picnic in Italy.

What...
Che...

> **craziness!**
> *casino!*
>
> **a disaster!**
> *disastro!*

madness!
pasticcio!

a shame!
peccato!

a scam!
imbroglio!

a scene!
chiassata!

a bitch!
bordello!
Literally, "brothel."

trouble!
guaio!

Shut your trap!
Chiudi il becco!

There's an old Latin expression, *silentium est aurum* ("Silence is golden"). It's harder to take something back than to avoid saying the wrong thing at the wrong time. When five people are talking at the same time, and you've had it with all the talking, use these *espressioni* to get through to your yapping friends. Variations of the word *zitto* are used to tell someone to zip it.

Be quiet!
Taci!

Shut up, dickhead!
Sta' zitto, testa di cazzo!

Hear me out.
Ascoltami.

Listen.
Senti.

Come on!
Di'!

Pay attention to me.
Dammi retta.

Shut your trap!
Chiudi il becco!
Literally, "Close your beak."

Spill it!
Dimmi!

Tell me everything.
Dimmi tutto.

Best wishes!
Auguri!

Even if you're depressed, have run out of Prozac, and are feeling slightly suicidal, it never helps to dwell. Put on your best smile and *celebrare* every chance you can.

Congrats!
Congratulazioni!

Happy birthday!
Buon compleanno!

Happy holidays!
Buone feste!

Well done!
Ben fatto!

Awesome!
Mitico!

Charming!
Grazioso!

WHO?
CHI?

You don't have to speak perfect Italian to get by—these little question words can help you score a lot of points. After all, you've got to know *dove* (where) and *quando* (when) it's time to meet up.

Who is that hot babe?
***Chi** è quella figa?*

Where do we know each other from?
***Ci** conosciamo?*

What the fuck are you doing?
***Che** cazzo fai?*
Che cosa is also used to mean "what" in a lot of cases.

Why don't we have a quickie right here?
***Perché** non ci facciamo una sveltina qui in questo momento?*

How do you like it?
***Come** ti piace?*

Wait! You've done it with **how many** people?
*Aspetta! Con **quante** persone l'hai fatto?*

Compliments!
Complimenti!

Fabulous!
Favoloso!

Fantastic!
Fantastico!

Sweet!
Che figata!

Way to go!
Eh vai!

What a blast!
Che bomba!

CHAPTER **2**

Friends & Flirting

Gli Amici & Flirtare

The best way to learn friendly Italian is to sit at the nearest café and listen to the melodious chitter-chatter. Italians are known for their banter, where ribbing, gossiping, and teasing are all forms of demonstrating their affection for both friends and *famiglia*. Italians don't beat around the bush—if they want to know you better, they'll ask you for all sorts of personal *informazione*. Be prepared to answer, and don't hold back if you have a question or two yourself. Being direct is appreciated (most of the time).

Friends or f-buddies?

Amici o trombamici?

You might be an island of *indipendenza* and self-reliance, but Italians like to really connect. They hang out in *gruppi* and make new friends through existing ones. This works out well for foreigners, because once you've made the acquaintance of one Italian, it's only a matter of time before you're warming up to his or her entire clan.

Do you like unicorns? We have so much in common. Let's be friends.
Ti piacciono gli unicorni? Abbiamo tanto in comune. Facciamo amicizia.

He/She's....
Lui/Lei è....

a friend
un amico/un'amica

a close friend
un amico/un'amica d'intimo

a really tight friend
un amico/un'amica di ferro
Literally, "an iron friend."

my best friend
il mio migliore amico/la mia migliore amica

my BFF
il mio amico/la mia amica del cuore
Literally, "friend of the heart."

my blood
il mio amico/la mia amica per la pelle
Literally, "my skin friend."

a bosom buddy
un amico/un'amica cilegia
Literally, "a cherry friend," from the fact that when you pick cherries, they come in pairs.

a soulmate
un'anima gemella
Literally, "a twin soul."

my fuck-buddy
il mio compagno/la mia compagna di trombate

a friend with benefits
un po' più di un amico/un'amica
Literally, "a little more than a friend."

a buddy
un/a compagno/a

a roommate
un/a compagno/a di camera

a classmate
un/a compagno/a di scuola

playmate
un/a compagno/a di giochi

a domestic partner
un/a convivente

a pen pal
un amico/un'amica di penna

an acquaintance
un/una conoscente

a coworker
un/a collega

a frenemy
un amico/un'amica del giaguaro
Literally, "a jaguar friend," someone who pretends to be your friend but is really a two-timer who gets off on duping you.

Hey, dude
Ciao, amico

Although there doesn't appear to be a universally accepted translation of "Hey, dude" in Italian, it's safe to say *Ciao, amico* ("Hi, friend") is a pretty close fit. In different dialects, Italians also throw around *ciccio* (Tuscany), *zio* (Milan), *cumpà* (southern Italy), or *cocco* (Central Italy). In the good old days, many Italian-American communities used *paesan* (short for *paesano*) to indicate a buddy or mate. These aren't the old days. Best to stick with *amico* or *fratello*.

Bro
Fra'

Brother
Fratello
Literally, "brother," but also used to indicate a friend.

How's it goin', **homey**?
*Come va, **compagno**?*
Compagno is literally "countryman."

Hey, **friend**!
*Ciao, **amico**!*
Amico is also used to address someone as dude.

That **dude** at the club was so whack.
*Quel **tipo** al club era folle.*

I met some **guy** whose name I can't remember.
*Ho conosciuto un **tizio** il cui nome non mi ricordo.*

How's life treating you, **pal**?
*Come ti va la vita, **compare**?*
Compaesano is also used.

Family
La famiglia

In Italy, you must *avere un appuntamento* to "make a date" to go out with someone. Serial dating is considered bad form to most Italians. You don't test drive people to see if they're to your liking. Your first date with an Italian could well involve an *introduzione* to the entire clan. If you make the grade, you can have a second date. Here's a little tip to remember: Never *arrivare* at someone's home empty-handed, even if they tell you otherwise. Etiquette says it's polite to always bring pastries, *una bottiglia di vino*, or some hand-picked *fiori* (flowers)...anything to show your appreciation.

Father
Padre

Daddy
Papà
The final accented *à* should be stressed to distinguish it from the word *Papa* (as in the Pope); this is also not to be confused with the word *pappa* (baby mush).

Pops
Babbo

Mother
Madre

Mom
Mamma

Husband
Marito

Wife
Moglie

Brother/little brother
Fratello/fratellino

Sister/little sister
Sorella/sorellina

Fiancé
Fidanzato/a
Even if you're not planning to tie the knot anytime soon, the term *fidanzato/a* (fiancé/fiancée) is used to describe your special squeeze, a vestige from the old days.

Cousin
Cugino/a

Uncle/Aunt
Zio/a

Auntie
Comare
This is the "auntie" that's not really related but gets the title anyway, and is used for close family friends as well. This is technically dialect; it's commonly heard in movies and among Italian-American families.

Family friend
Amico/a di famiglia

Single parent
Gengle
From a combination of the word *genitori*, meaning parents, and the word "single."

Chromosome X
Cromosoma X

La femmina (female) comes in all shapes and sizes, but after centuries of war and peace (and a Renaissance and an Enlightenment, as well), the iconic *Italiana* has nurtured and cultivated an attitude that comes across in everything she does. She takes no prisoners—buyer beware.

A chica
Una tipa giusta

A chick
Una fanciulla

A gal
Una tipa

A girl
Una ragazza

A good girl
Una ragazza tutta casa e chiesa
Literally, "a girl who is all home and church."

A nice girl
Una buona

A saint
Una santa
A variation of *santa*, *santina* is also used in the sarcastic expression *faccia da santina senza aureola* ("face of a little saint without the halo").

A schoolgirl
Uno zainetto
Zainetto refers to the *zaino* (backpack) that all teenage girls carry.

A sweet girl
Una ragazza acqua e sapone
Literally, "a girl who's soap and water."

A blabbermouth
Una chiacchierona

A single mother
Una ragazza madre

A cougar
Una tardona

An old lady
Una vecchia signora

A wild thing
Una selvaggia

A man-eater
Una iena
Literally, "a hyena."

A wild horse
Una cavalla

A witch
Una strega

Chromosome Y
Cromosoma Y

Il maschio italiano isn't as easy to define as stereotyping would have you believe. He's even an enigma to himself.

A boy
Un ragazzo

An unlucky bastard
Un poveraccio

A sugar daddy
Un papà-amante

A newbie
Un giovane
This term refers to someone inexperienced.

An animal
Un animale

A beast
Una bestia

A boy toy
Un uomo più giovane

A Casanova
Un uomo galante

A gigolo
Un gigolò

A Guido
Un birro
Incidentally, in Italy, Guido is simply a name.

A baller
Un donnaiolo

A playboy
Uno stallone
Literally, "a stallion."

A pimp
Un magnaccio/a

A player
Un ganzo

A jock
Un tipo sportivo

MOMISM
IL MAMMISMO

Il mammismo is a decidedly Italian concept that refers to the tendency of unmarried adult male children to remain dependent on their mommies for most of their domestic needs. Extremely high youth unemployment and limited digs are mostly to blame for the fact that more than 50 percent of Italian males aged 18 to 34 still live at *casa*, yet no one seems to mind too much. (The same for most unmarried females, but their mothers probably aren't doing their laundry.) If you're an American guy dating an Italian girl, you'll win a lot of points just by the fact you have been conditioned to take your own *piatto* (plate) to the sink and actually wash your own stinking underwear.

Sure, he's cute, but what a **mamma's boy**.
*Sì, lui è carino, ma che **mammone**.*

What a crybaby!
Che figlio di mamma!

A metrosexual
Un metrosessuale

A mooch
Uno scroccone

A pussy
Un coniglio
Literally, "a rabbit."

A sex maniac
Un maniaco sessuale

A tough cookie
Un tipo tosto

A trickster
Un truffatore

Animals

Gli animali

Speaking of *la famiglia*, Italians love their *animali domestici* (pets) almost as much as they love their *bambini*.

What is your **dog/cat/bird** called?
Come si chiama il tuo ***cane/gatto/uccello****?*

How old is your dog/cat?
Quanti anni ha *il tuo cane/gatto?*

I go **crazy** for animals!
Vado ***matto/a*** *per gli animali!*

I take my dog out for a walk every day.
Porto fuori il cane ogni giorno.

Cute dog!
Che bel cane!

Shit! I stepped in shit.
Merda*! Ho fatto un passo nella merda!*

Damn dog!
Maledetto *cane!*

Stop **humping** my leg!
Basta con lo ***sbattermi*** *la gamba!*

Don't **pee** on the rug!
Non ***pisciare*** *sul tappetto!*

I've got pet hair all over.
Ci sono dei peli dappertutto.

Where can I find a **lint brush**?
Dove posso ottenere un ***pannello per i peli****?*

I'm allergic to **cats.**
Sono allergico/a ai ***gatti.***

Where can I get some **anthistamines**?
Dove posso trovare un ***antistaminico****?*

When you're at the Foro Romano, you can leave your leftovers for the many cats that call Rome home. *I gatti liberi* (free cats) have the same rights as any sentient being in Italy, and were officially acknowledged in 1991 by the *il codice del gatto libero* ("the free cat law").

Here **kitty**, want some leftover spaghetti?
Vieni qui ***micio****, ne vuoi degli spaghetti?*

Social creatures
Creature sociali

When you come across certain humans, it's almost as if there were animals.

He/She is such....
Lui/lei è proprio....

a partier
un festaiolo

a party animal
animale da festa

a fun person
un buontempone

a pleasure seeker
un gaudente

a binge drinker
un vitaiolo

a show-off
un animale da palcoscenico

a natural
un talento naturale

the queen of the ball
la regina della festa

Characters

I tipi

A punk (related to music)
Un/a punk

A rocker
Un/a rockettaro/a

A hick
Un/a campagnolo/a

A hippie
Un/a hippie

A hustler
Un/a imbroglione/a

A fucker
Un fottitore/una fottitrice

A phoney
Un/a falsone/a

A gold digger
Un cacciatore/una cacciatrice di dote

A goody-two shoes
Uno/a che tiene un piede in due scarpe
Literally, "someone who keeps one foot in two shoes."

A gossip
Un/a pettegolo/a

A wet blanket
Un/a guastafeste

A dork
Un secchione
Literally, "a bucket."

A loser
Uno/a sfigato/a
Depending on context, this word gets a lot of mileage; it can also mean "nerd" or "dork."

A tool
Un/a imbranato/a

A party pooper
Un/a noiosone/a

A deadbeat
Uno sgarbato

He's got real **guts.**
Ha proprio ***fegato.***
Fegato literally means "liver." It's a compliment.

Flirting
Flirtare

In the old days, a single young woman was called *nubile*, while an unwed male was referred to as *celibe* (from "celibate"). Once the strays started growing on her unmarried chin, she became *una zitella* (an old maid); when his ears sprouted hair, he was simply deemed *uno scapolo* (a bachelor). Today, Italians simply describe themselves as either *sposato/a* (married) or *non sposato/a* (not married). The English word "single" is also used, but with an Italian accent it would sound more like *SEEN-gol.*

Do you live **alone**?
Vivi da ***solo/a****?*

Do you have a partner?
Hai un/a partner?

Are you **married**?
Sei ***sposato/a****?*

This is **my boyfriend**.
*Questo è **il mio ragazzo**.*

This is **my girlfriend**.
*Questo è **la mia ragazza**.*

About Italian grammar and possessives: The "my" part reflects the gender of the thing that is being possessed. *Il mio* (my) is used in front of masculine nouns. *La mia* (my) is used in front of feminine nouns.

We're basically **engaged**.
*Siamo praticamente **fidanzati**.*

I'm ....
Sono....

single
single

married
sposato/a

separated
separato/a

divorced
divorziato/a

widowed
vedovo/a

I'm yours.
Sono tuo/tua.

This is....
Questo/a è....

my lover
il mio/la mia amante

my sweetheart
il mio/la mia innamorato/a

my man
il mio uomo

my woman
la mia donna

my partner
il mio/la mia partner
Compagno/a is also used.

We've been **together** for five months.
Siamo ***insieme*** *da cinque mesi.*

How old are you?
Quanti anni hai?

Why are you so interested?
Perché interessa a te?

He loves me...he loves me not
Mi ama...non mi ama

It's *l'amore a prima vista*...love at first sight. The endorphins have kicked in and you're over-the-top *innamorato* (in love). When this happens with an Italian, there is no limit to how totally hokey you can get. Go ahead and gush. Life's too short to hold back.

I love you!
Ti amo!

I love you to death!
Ti amo *da morire!*

Let's make love.
Facciamo *l'amore.*

I care about you like no one else.
Tengo a te *come non tengo a nessun altro.*

If you take my hand, **we'll go far**.
Prendendomi la mano, ***noi andremo lontano***.

I'm madly in love with you!
Ti amo alla follia!

I need you!
Ho bisogno di te!

You are the **light** in my eyes.
*Tu sei la **luce** dei miei occhi.*

You have **bewitched** me.
*Mi hai **stregato/a**.*

You are the man/woman of my **dreams**!
*Sei l'uomo/la donna dei miei **sogni**!*

For you **I'd do anything**.
*Per te **farei di tutto**.*

For love or force.
Per amore o per forza.
Used to describe something inevitable.

You and me **forever**.
*Io e te per **sempre**.*

You're my **everything**.
*Sei il mio **tutto**.*

I can't **live** without you!
*Non posso **vivere** senza di te!*

I think about you all the time.
***Ti penso** sempre.*

There's **only** you.
*C'è **solo** te.*

You're **incredible**!
*Sei **incredible**!*

I'm yours **forever**.
*Sono il tuo/la tua per **sempre**.*

You're my **soul mate**.
*Sei la mia **anima gemella**.*
Literally, "twin soul"—isn't that adorable?

I hope **our story** never ends.
Spero che ***la nostra storia*** *non finisca mai.*

You are my **life**.
Sei la mia ***vita****.*

You are my **rose**.
Sei la mia ***rosa****.*

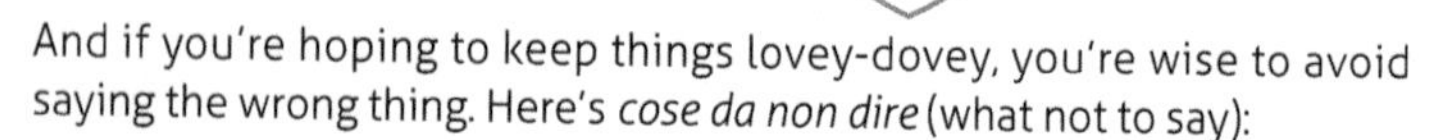

And if you're hoping to keep things lovey-dovey, you're wise to avoid saying the wrong thing. Here's *cose da non dire* (what not to say):

You remind me of my ex.
Assomigli a una mia ex.

Can you loan me five bucks/Euros?
Mi puoi prestare cinque dollari/Euro?

Are you also **blonde** down there?
Sei ***bionda*** *anche sotto?*

I just got into town, how about a rain check?
Sono appena arrivato/a, un'altra volta?

When things don't work out
Quando le cose non vanno

It's easy to *innamorarsi* (to fall in love), but it can be devastating to discover that all those sweet words were saccharin-coated crud. Whether your lover is male or female, discovering your trust has been misused can take a long time to overcome. But sometimes, rejection is protection. Better to be alone than with the wrong *persona*. And there's always make-up sex, called *fare pace a letto* (to make peace in bed).

We broke up.
Ci siamo separati.

She/he broke my **heart**.
Mi ha rotto il ***cuore****.*

My girlfriend dumped me.
La mia ragazza *mi ha mollato.*

My boyfriend left me.
Il mio ragazzo *mi ha lasciata.*

We split a month ago.
Ci siamo lasciati *un mese fa.*

I can't eat, sleep, or think.
Non posso *mangiare, dormire, o pensare.*

I'll **never** love again.
Non mi innamorerò ***mai*** *più.*

Sorry, but you're not **my type**.
Scusami, ma non sei ***il mio tipo/la mia tipa.***

The art of seduction
L'arte della seduzione

The caricature of the Italian man pounding his hirsute chest King Kong–style is an insulting, outdated stereotype. Today's typical Italian male is well dressed and stylish, and if he's wearing eyeglasses, they are most certainly designer. What hasn't changed is the fact that an Italian man will do anything to get a woman's *attenzione*. He'll tell her she's the most *bella, interessante* woman he's ever met...that he's never felt this way before...that he's been waiting for her *tutta la vita* (his entire life). She may know he's full of shit and will more than likely laugh in his face, but if the *passione* is mutual and *la luna* hits like a big pizza pie, then that's *amore*. So move in bro, and give it your best shot.

Day and night **I think only of you**.
Giorno e notte ***penso solo a te.***

Don't tell me your name, **just kiss me**.
Non dirmi il tuo nome, ***baciami e basta.***

Wanna see my **tattoo**?
*Vuoi vedere il mio **tatuaggio**?*

I'm **crazy** about you!
*Sono **pazzo** di te!*

Without you there's no sun in the sky.
Senza di te non c'è sole in cielo.

You are **my obsession**.
*Sei la **mia ossessione**.*

I can't think about anything but you.
Non faccio altro che pensare a te.

I get lost in your **eyes**.
*Mi perdo nei tuoi **occhi**.*

Marry me or I'll die!
***Sposami** o morirò!*

There's a hole inside me that only you can fill.
***C'è un vuoto dentro di me** che solo tu puoi colmare.*

You are **the most beautiful woman** I've ever seen.
*Tu sei **la donna più bella** che io abbia mai visto.*

You have stolen my **heart**.
*Mi hai rubato il **cuore**.*

You're the only one.
Sei l'unica.

Your eyes are like **diamonds**.
*I tuoi occhi sono come **brillanti**.*

You have **enchanted** me.
*Mi hai **incantato/a**.*

I'm so **horny** for you!
*Sono **arrapatissimo** per te!*

Help me, **I'm desperate**!
*Aiutami, **sono disperato**!*

I want to smooch you.
Voglio pomiciarti.

You have **luscious lips**.
*Hai le **labbra squisite**.*

If you didn't exist, I'd have to invent you.
Se non ci fossi dovrei inventarti.

You are a **jewel**.
*Sei un **gioiello**.*

Be happy, be gay
Sta' bene, sta' gay

There are gay and lesbian *comunità* in the major *città* like Venezia, Milano, Firenze, and Roma, with smaller (and harder to find) enclaves outside. Be discreet: A lot of Italian gays keep things on the down-low, so don't go outing someone by accident. Italian gays, when they're ready, use the English term "coming out," as well as the Italian *essere allo scoperto* (to be discovered), to describe the process.

Italy's national gay rights organizations Arcigay and Arcilesbica (www.arcigay.it and www.arcilesbica.com) supported the coming out movement, F.U.O.R.I. (Fronte Unitario Omosessuale Rivoluzionario Italiano, whose acronym means "out"). Members receive membership cards that can be used in participating gay bookstores, clubs, and bars. *Il matrimonio gay* is probably a bit far away for the conservatively minded, mostly Catholic country.

He/She is....
Lui/Lei è....

> **straight**
> *uno/a straight*
>
> **bisexual**
> *bisessuale*

bicurious
bicuriosa

queer
una checca
The English word "queer" is also used.

gay
un gay

homosexual
un omosessuale

a homo
un omosex

a queen
una regina

an auntie
una zietta

a catcher
un orecchione
Literally, "big ear." This is very insulting. It's sweeter euphemism is *ricchione.*

a fruitcake
uno/a suonato/a nella testa
This one is pretty offensive, so be careful when using it.

transgender (m.)
un transgender

transsexual (m.)
un transessuale

transvestite (m.)
un travestito

a lesbian
una lesbica
The term *saffismo* is also used to describe lesbianism, from the Greek lyricist and poet Sappho (c. 620–570 BC), born on the island of Lesbos.

a lesbo
una lesbo

a dyke
una lesbicona

Where can we go **cruising**?
Dove possiamo fare il ***battuage****?*

I can't stand **homophobia**.
Non sopporto ***l'omofobia****.*

You're safe with me.
Sei al sicuro/a *con me.*

Let's keep this between us for now, **okay**?
Teniamocelo per noi per il momento, ***va bene****?*

You're so cool!
Sei in gamba!

Use these adjectives to describe someone to your BFF.

He/She is....
Lui/Lei è....

cool
in gamba

fun
divertente

funny
buffo/a

silly
sciocco/a

clever
furbo/a

friendly
amichevole

nice
gentile

sweet
dolce

generous
generoso/a

simple
semplice

laid-back
alla mano

cultured
colto/a

spirited
spiritoso/a

captivating
accattivante

delightful
delizioso/a

fascinating
affascinante

CHAPTER 3

Booze, Bars, & Clubs

Gli Alcolici, I Bar, & I Club

You'll find there's no lack of opportunities to party in Italy, whether it's *Natale* (Christmas), New Year's, someone's *compleanno* (birthday), or just *perché* (because). It seems like there are more holidays per year than regular days. Italians also celebrate their *onomastico* (name day), honoring the saint whose name they share. (If your name is Dweezel, you'll probably have to invent your own.)

Going out

Uscire

Do you wanna go out tonight?
Vuoi uscire *stasera?*

Come on, **let's party**!
Dai, ***facciamo festa****!*

Let's go.
Andiamo.
Andiamo means both "let's go" and "we're going." If the only exposure you've had to the Italian language is through *What They Didn't Teach You In Italian Class*, understanding how to use this verb will help you a lot.

I'm not feeling up for it tonight.
Non mi va per stasera.

Tonight I'm staying home to watch **my favorite TV show**.
Stasera rimango a casa a guardare ***il mio programmna preferito****.*

Move your ass. **Let's roll.**
Alza il culo. ***Usciamo.***

Don't be such a **lame-o**, come on.
Non essere ***una palla****, dai.*
Literally, "don't be a ball."

What do you say we go...?
Perché non andiamo...?

> **dancing**
> *a ballare*
>
> **for a walk**
> *a fare un giro*
>
> **get drunk**
> *ubriacarci*
>
> **have something to eat/drink**
> *a prendere qualcosa da mangiare/bere*
>
> **listen to music**
> *ad ascoltare la musica*
>
> **watch a movie**
> *a guardare un film*
>
> **see a show**
> *a vedere uno spettacolo*

Let's go....
Andiamo....

> **to the pub**
> *al pub*
>
> **to the bar**
> *al bar*
>
> **to the club**
> *in discoteca*
>
> **to that party you were talking about**
> *a quella festa di cui parlavi*

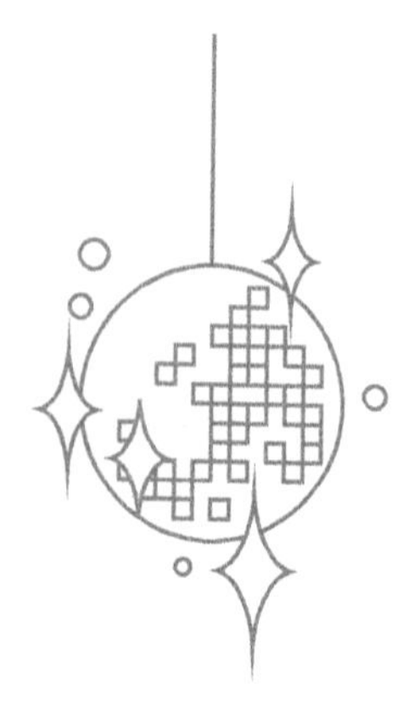

anywhere
dovunque

around
in giro

Where's the **party** at?
Dove sta la ***festa*** *oggi?*

This place is....
Questo posto è....

boring
noioso

busy
affollato

packed
pienissimo

awesome
grande
Literally, "big."

crazy
pazzesco

off the hook
in voga

lame
palloso

dead
morto

I've got two tickets to a rave.
Ho due flyer per un rave party.

It's overrated.
È uno schianto.

The party was bumping.
Era pazzesca la festa.

What a **shithole.**
*Che **merdaio.***

This place is not happening.
Non succede niente qui.

I've had it. Let's go.
***Sono stufo/a.** Andiamo.*

I can't stay here any longer.
Non ci sto più dentro.

Drinking
Il bere

Italians hang out in bars from morning till night, but not necessarily to drink themselves into a satisfied stupor. In Italy, *il bar* refers to both a bar and a café. *Il pub* is the best place to go for a *birra.*

Can I get you **something to drink?**
*Posso offrirti **qualcosa da bere?***

How about a **glass of wine?**
*Ti va un **bicchiere di vino?***

Red or white?
Rosso o bianco?

Can I order a **carafe** of the house wine?
*Ti va una **caraffa** del vino di casa?*

What do you have **on tap?**
*Che cosa avete **alla spina?***

I'll take a **bottle of water.**
*Prenderò **una bottiglia di acqua.***
Italian tap water is completely potable, so if you're not into spending three bucks on a bottle of water, just ask for *acqua normale,* or "normal water."

Chug it! Chug it!
Dai! Bevi!
When Italians *fare un brindisi* (make a toast), they'll say *cin cin* or *saluti!*

Why don't we...?
Perché non...?

take **a shot** of tequila
*beviamo **un sorso** di tequila*

take **some shots**
*beviamo **dei cicchetti***

order a bottle of prosecco
***ordinare** una bottigila di prosecco*

knock back a few
***prendere qualcosa** da bere*

Do you want **some bubbly**?
*Vuoi **dello spumante**?*

This whiskey is totally **watered down**.
*Questo whiskey è completamente **annacquato**.*

I'll take **a cold beer**.
*Prendo **una birra fredda**.*

La birra is also very good in Italy. If you're over 18 and can't legally drink in the States, welcome to *Italia!*

Give me **a pint**.
*Dammi **una pinta**.*

What a **shitty beer**.
*Che **birra di merda**.*

Drinking to excess
Prendersi una sbronza

While the Italians are no strangers to excess and extravagance, the expression *prendersi una sbronza* (taking on stupidity) refers to getting tanked. Wisen up: Although their language possesses as many terms for inebriation as there are means to get you there, Italians rarely go out just to get wasted. Tequila and other hard liquors are sometimes referred to as *benzina agricola* (agricultural fuel).

There's a big difference between *bevuto di bello* (happy drunk) and *bevuto di brutto* (ugly drunk, equivalent to shit-faced), though the transition between the two may be only a couple of glasses of *prosecco*, the Italian equivalent of champagne. *L'eccessiva indulgenza* (overindulgence) is not anything to be proud of; you definitely don't want anyone Snapchatting your naked ass.

I'm so....
Sono....

That foreign-exchange student is....
Quello studente straniero è....

buzzed
sballato/a

tipsy
brillo/a

I HAD A HELLUVA OF A TIME
MI SONO DIVERTITO/A UN BORDELLO!

After the party is over, Italians love to relive the event by talking about how great it was. You can substitute any of the following to express this. The translations don't always work in English, so I've given you the literal meaning.

I had a helluva of...!
Mi sono divertito/a...!

a brothel	*un bordello*
a whole lot	*un casino*
a fortune	*una cifra*
a beating	*un fracco*
a pile	*un puttanaio*
a sack	*un sacco*

sloshed
inzuppato/a

drunk
ubriaco/a

drunk as a skunk
ubriaco come una scimmia
Literally, "drunk as a monkey."

messed up
massacrato/a

completely shit-faced
rincoglionito/a
Literally, "made stupid."

destroyed
distrutto/a

gone
andato/a

hammered
da buttare

out of it
rovinato/a
Literally, "ruined."

plastered
demolito/a
Literally, "demolished."

trashed
trashato/a

fucked up
devastato/a
Literally, "devastated."

Check out that punk! He's totally **smashed**.
Guarda quel punk! Lui è completamente ***fatto****.*

The students were **wasted off their asses.**
Gli studenti erano ***sbronzi fino all'osso.***
Literally, "drunk to the bone."

Alberto drinks **like a fish.**
Alberto beve ***come una spugna.***
Literally, "like a sponge."

You're an **alcoholic.**
Sei ***alcolizzato/a.***

Baked
Ciucco

Toasted, baked, blazed...here are a few more terms thrown around that describe party animals.

High
Fuori
Literally, "out."

Totaled
Duro fuori
The expression *Duro fuori fragile dentro* translates to "tough on the outside, soft on the inside."

Toasted
Stravolto/a

Blazed
Allegro/a

Baked
Ciucco/a

Faded
Spento come un fiammifero
Literally, "out like a match."

Ripped
Schizzato/a

Tweaking
In paranoia

Stoned
Fumato/a

Tripping
Pasticcato/a

A drug addict
Un tossicodipendente

A junkie
Un tossico

Smokin'
Il fumo

Believe it or not, *il fumare* (smoking) is now prohibited in most indoor establishments and public spaces in Italy. Tobacco can be purchased at the *tabaccheria* (tobacco shop) and in many bars. A minority of Italians smoke a combination of hash (or weed) and tobacco. A *purino* is pure reefer and is rarely smoked.

Do you smoke?
Fumi?

Can I bum a **smoke**?
*Posso fregarti una **siga**?*

Can you **light** me up?
*Hai d'**accendere**?*

Do you have **rolling papers**?
*Hai un **papier**?*

Is it okay if I smoke a **cigarette**?
*Va bene se fumo una **sigaretta**?*

Drugs
La droga

Italian laws are harsh when it comes to illegal drugs, whether you're talking about cocaine, heroin, hashish, or marijuana. Even recreational use is considered excessive. I don't know about you, but I'll have a glass of *vino* instead. There are certainly better places to spend my time than inside an Italian *prigione* (prison).

Marijuana
La marijuana

Ganja
La gangia

Grass
Il basilico
Literally, "basil."

Herb
L'erba

Maryjane
La Maria

Pot
La roba

A doobie
Un flower

A hit
Un tiro

> Go on, **take a hit.**
> *Dai, **tira**.*

A joint
Una canna/un spinello

> Mind if I light up a **joint**?
> *Mi faccio una **canna**?*

A spliff
Una fiamma
Literally, "flame."

A twist
Una paglia
Literally, "straw," like hay...not the kind you snort with.

He's such a chain-smoking pothead.
Quello ha fumato l'ombra di un bosco.
Literally, "He smoked the shadow of a forest."

Cocaine
La cocaina

Blow
La bomba
Literally, "bomb."

Coke
La coca

A line
Un colpo
Literally, "a hit."

Ectasy
Le pasticchette di ecstasy

Give me a **pill.**
Dammi una ***pasta.***
The word *pasta* in this case refers to any mind-altering pill such as ecstasy. Also used are the words *pasticca*, *chicca*, and *trip*.

Hungover
Sbronzo

The Italians and their ancestors have been partying for a long time, since around 200 BC. The *baccanalia* were the ecstatic, mystical festivals based on the Bacchus cult. Nothing short of an unruly frat party, drinking games included sucking down as many cups of wine as indicated by the throw of *i dadi* (the dice). Contrary to popular thinking, the Romans did not have separate vomit rooms for this purpose.

Amazingly, Italian does not have a precise term for "hangover." You can say *il dopo-sbornia* (the after plaster) and *dopo-sbronzo* (after the party), but these still aren't quite the same as the English (which is not to say Italians don't get hungover).

Dude, is everything okay?
***Amico**, tutto okay?*

I drank way to much last night.
***Ho bevuto** troppo ieri notte.*

I feel like **shit.**
*Mi sento come la **merda**.*

I'm so **hungover.**
*Sono proprio **sbronzo/a**.*

I got totally plastered last night.
***Mi sono preso una bella sbornia** ieri notte.*

Do you have any aspirin? I've got a **killer headache.**
*Hai della aspirina? Ho un brutto **mal di testa**.*

My head is about to **explode.**
*La testa sta per **esplodere**.*

I'm **nauseous.**
*Mi sento la **nausea**.*

I have the **spins**.
Mi ***gira*** *la testa.*

He **vomited** all night.
Ha ***vomitato*** *tutta la notte.*

Cops
La pula

You can easily spot the *carabinieri*, Italy's military police, not to be confused with the local *polizia* (police). They're the uniformed studs you see in airports and *stazioni* with big guns slung over their broad shoulders. Their job, aside from protecting the country from *terroristi*, is to scare the *crapola* out of you. They're not like the friendly, fuzzy-headed Buckingham Palace guards who won't even blink if you crap on their shoes. That said, most *carabinieri* are still going home to *mamma* when the day is done.

The **police** are coming!
Arriva ***la polizia****!*

Fuzz
Gli sbirri

Pigs
I piedipiatti
Literally, "flatfoots."

Police officer
Il poliziotto/la poliziotta

Po-po
Lo sgherro

Traffic cop
Il vigile/la vigilessa

CHAPTER **4**

Sexy Body, Ugly Body

Il Corpo Bello & Brutto

Italians have a funny habit of *fissando lo sguardo* (staring each other down) when they're out walking. Unlike North Americans, they feel no *compulsione* to acknowledge the fact that you exist. Without apology, they'll scan you *dalla testa ai piedi* (from head to toe). Chances are you've been assessed, dissed, and dismissed before the scent of their cologne or *profumo* (perfume) has even caught up with you. *La soluzione*: Learn how to stare back. Not with those beady eyes—the stare should be unapologetic, piercing, and deadpan, no emotions attached.

Nice body!
Che corpo!

You are....
Tu sei....

He/She is....
Lui/Lei è....

> **cute**
> *carino/a*
>
> **attractive**
> *attraente*
>
> **beautiful**
> *bello/a*

fine
togo/a

gorgeous
bellissimo/a

boyish/girlish
fanciullesco/a

in shape
in forma

muscular
muscoloso/a

bangin'
provocante

sexy
sexy

stylish
di moda

Your girlfriend is a total...!
La tua ragazza è veramente una...!

babe
bona

bombshell
bella strada di montagna
Literally, "a nice mountain road," referring to a woman with curves.

knock-out
sventola
Literally, "a slap."

MILF
mamma da scopare

real woman
vera donna

well-built woman
maggiorata

SUPER HOT!
FICHISSIMO!

For him: It's worth mentioning that *un fico* isn't just a fig. Also pronounced *figo*, the term refers to a very attractive Italian male, the kind that makes you suck in your breath and start shakin' your hand up and down. There are a few variations used along this theme for both sexes.

For her: The general terms *fica* and *figa* are used to describe a really hot chick. But wait a hot second before you start flinging these words around someone's daughter: Remember that *fica* also refers to a woman's genitalia, so use it with caution. Better yet, avoid using *fica* altogether.

Man! He is such...!
Caspita! Lui è proprio...!

a dream
un incanto

a babe
uno bono

a hunk
un fusto

a real man
un uomo vero

a stud
un fichetto
From the word *fico*.

She is **smokin' hot!**
Lei è ***fighissima!***

Bradley Cooper is one of the **sexiest men in the world.**
Bradley Cooper è uno degli ***uomini più sexy del mondo.***

I want a man who is **tall, dark, and handsome.**
*Voglio un uomo **bel tenebroso**.*

He's/She's got....
Lui/Lei ha....

a **nice** body
*un **bel** corpo*

a **hot** bod
*un corpo **provocante***

an attractive look
un bell'aspetto

a decent physique
un fisico niente male

a really cute **belly button**
*un **ombelico** molto carino*

killer **legs**
*le **gambe** da morire*

Ugly as sin
Brutto come un peccato

Not everyone is a walking version of *Venere* (Venus) or *Marte* (Mars).

Hot damn! You're....
***Ammazza!** Sei....*

If you ask me, he's/she's....
***Secondo me**, è....*

kinda funny looking
un po' strano/a

heinous
bruttissimo/a

chubby
ciccio/a (also *ciccione*)

fat
grassoccio/a

hairy
peloso/a

bald
calvo/a

bug-eyed
occhi a palla
Literally, "eyes of a ball."

gap-toothed
sdentato/a

smelly
puzzolente

He's/she's ugly as...
Lui/lei è brutto/a come...

a toad
un rospo

hunger
la fame

sin
il peccato

a demon
il demonio

the devil
il diavolo

Her/his good looks are only skin deep.
Ha la bellezza dell'asino.
Literally, "She/he's got beauty of an ass." The donkey refers to someone whose good looks are the result of being young.

Your sister is so **ugly** that if she tried to become a **whore**, she'd have to pay the clients.
Tua sorella è così ***brutta*** *che se va a fare la* ***puttana****, è lei che deve pagare i clienti.*
Attenzione: Insult someone's sister at your own risk.

Boobs
Le bocce

Boobies, tits, melons, pebbles—just like in English, Italian has tons of euphemisms for breasts. The most common terms are *il seno* (chest) and *le tette* (tits).

Can I **touch** your...?
Posso ***toccare****...?*

Do you want to touch my...?
Vuoi *toccare...?*

bust
il petto

hooters
le poppe

breasts
il seno

rack
il balcone
Literally, "balcony."

milk cans
le colombe
Literally, "doves."

mams
le mammelle

jugs
le melanzane
Literally, "eggplants."

melons
i meloni

Dina's **stacked.**
*Dina **è una maggiorata**.*

Wow, what a **huge rack**!
*Mamma mia, che **tette enormi**!*

Maria is **flat chested**, but she's really sexy.
*Maria ha **poco seno**, ma è molto sexy.*

YOU'RE TOO SKINNY!
SEI TROPPO MAGRA!

It's an understatement to say that Italians are comfortable talking about their bodies. Maybe they just like making non-Italians blush, but there's hardly anything regarding the body that Italians won't discuss. And if you think everyone is so svelte just because they walk twenty miles a day, think again. Italians (especially of the female persuasion) are as obsessed with *dimagrire/ingrassare* (losing weight/ gaining weight) as Americans are. A typical *complimento* is to ask a friend if she recently lost weight. A double compliment is to say that someone has really gone too far.

Skinny
Magro/a

Scrawny
Pelle e ossa
Literally, "skin and bones."

I've **gained weight**.
*Sono **ingrassato/a**.*

No you haven't, you've **lost weight**.
*Non è vero, sei **dimagrito/a**.*

Don't **overdo it** now!
*Non **esagerare**!*

You're **skinny as a rail**!
*Sei **magro/a come un chiodo**!*
Literally, "skinny as a nail."

You're such a **liar.**
*Sei proprio un **bugiardo/a**.*

I wouldn't lie to you.
*Non ti **mentirei.***

She has **nipples** like saucers.
*Ha i **capezzoli** come piattini.*

Pamela Anderson has **round and firm** breasts.
*Pamela Anderson ha i seni **rotondi e sodi**.*

But they're not **real**.
*Ma non sono **veri**.*

Ass
Il culo

Whether you're talking about an ass, butt, bum, or badonkadonk, the most commonly heard term is *culo*. Add *-ne* and you have *culone* (big ass), some serious junk in the trunk. A sexy girl with a beautiful derriere would be described as *una bellesponde* (beautiful banks) because of their resemblance to the curves along a river (poetic, no?).

Tush
Il dedrio

Tail
Il posteriore

Butt
Il fracco

Caboose
Il fiocco
Literally, "bow."

Cheeks
I fondelli; le chiappe

Heinie
Il mazzo
Literally, "cluster."

ASS SPEAK
IL LINGUAGGIO DEL CULO

Il culo (ass) is a word used in a gazillion ways. The end piece of a loaf of bread or a block of cheese is called a *culo*, whereas *una culata* is a bump made with one's backside, like with a dance move (e.g., twerking).

There are a few ass-related *espressioni* worth grabbing, and of course, when taken literally they sound far worse than when actually used! *Un dito in culo* (a finger in the ass) is a pain in the ass. If someone lives in *il culo al mondo* (in the ass of the world) it means they live in the boonies. *Non ha freddo nel culo* (he doesn't have a cold ass) refers to someone who's flush with cash.

Che culo hai!
You're one lucky S.O.B.
Literally, "to have ass."

Mario is a total **ass kisser**.
Mario è propio un ***leccaculo****.*

You're shameless as an ass.
Hai la faccia peggio del culo.
Literally, "Your face is worse than your ass."

Bonnie and Clyde are **thick as thieves**.
Bonnie e Clyde sono ***culo e camicia****.*
Literally, "to be ass and shirt with someone."

I busted my ass finding you ice cream at this hour.
Mi sono fatto il culo *per trovarti il gelato a quest'ora.*

The project went **to shit**.
Il progetto è andato ***in culo****.*
Literally, "to go to the ass."

It seems like she's/he's got **eyes in the back of his/her head**.
Sembra che abbia gli ***occhi anche nel culo****.*
Literally, "to have eyes even in your ass."

Are you jerking me around?
Mi stai prendendo per il culo?
Literally, "to catch by the ass."

Get your ass in gear; we're late!
Alza il culo; siamo in ritardo!

What a stroke of luck!
Che botta di culo!
Literally, "What a hit of ass!"

Rear end
Il contrabbasso
Literally, "contrabass."

Rump
Il melone
Literally, "melon."

Bubble butt
Il balconcino
Literally, "balcony."

Cushion
Il pallone
Literally, "big ball."

Booty
Canestro
Like a "basket," also used to describe a basketball hoop.

Trunk
La tasca
Literally, "pocket."

Clean fun
Il divertimento pulito

When in a bather's paradise like Italy, do as the bathers do and steep yourself in one of the many *terme* (thermal baths) located throughout the country. There's no better way to check out the goods without making it too obvious. In the old days, you could go to *i bagni* (the bathhouses) to find all sorts of lustful pleasures. The *bagni di gruppo* (group baths) were popular among adulterous high-ranking men to get a little *bunga-bunga* on the side.

Feel free to soak up until you get pruney in these bath houses, but know that it's not so cool to take hour-long showers like you do back home. You'll use up all the *acqua calda* (hot water), you vulgar, oblivious, energy hog!

Let's go chill at the **spa.**
Andiamo a rilassarci al ***centro benessere.***
Literally, "well-being center."

The water's **hella hot/freezing.**
L'acqua è ***bollente/ghiacciata.***

I'd like....
Vorrei....

> **a nice massage**
> *un bel massaggio*
>
> **a manicure**
> *una manicure*
>
> **a pedicure**
> *una pedicure*
>
> **a facial**
> *un facciale*
>
> **a mud bath**
> *un bagno di fango*
>
> **a bathrobe**
> *un accappatoio*

Pissing and shitting
Il pisciare e il cagare

You may think you're hysterical playing "pull my finger," but some things are best kept private. The next time you bust ass, step on a duck, or cut a muffin, blame it on the dog.

Where's the **can?**
Dov'è il ***cesso****?*

I gotta....
Devo....

> go to the **bathroom**
> *andare in* ***bagno***
>
> go **pee**
> *fare la* ***pipì***

crap
cagare

BEAUTIFUL SHIT
BELLA MERDA

You're shit in luck, because the Italians use the word *merda* pretty much the same way English speakers use the word "shit." In addition, there are quite a few similar expressions related to scat. *Un pezzo di merda* refers to "a piece of shit," and *un sacco di merda* refers to "a sack of shit." And there's the ever-descriptive *merda per merda!* (Shit for shit!)

Enrico is a **shitface**.
Enrico ha una ***faccia di merda****.*

What a **shitty** film!
Che film di ***merda****!*

I'm up to my **neck** in shit.
Sono proprio nella merda fino al ***collo****!*

You're a real shit.
Sei *proprio una merda.*

What a **shithead!**
Che ***testa di merda****!*

What a **shithole.**
Che ***merdaio****.*

You make a **shitty impression** when you act like an **turd.**
Fai una ***figura di merda*** *quando ti comporti come uno* ***stronzo.***

You're in deep **shit**!
Sei nella ***merda****!*

Eat shit and **die**!
Mangia *merda e* ***muore****!*

Enjoy these shitty *proverbi* (proverbs):

If you **run while you shit,** you'll get shit all over yourself.
A ***correre*** *e* ***cagare,*** *ci si immerda i garretti.*
Used when you're trying to do too much at once.

If March throws **grass,** April throws **shit**.
Se marzo butta ***erba,*** *aprile butta* ***merda.***
The pessimistic version of "April showers bring May flowers."

I laughed so hard **I pissed** myself.
*Mi **sono pisciato** addosso dalle risate.*

Poop
Cacca

A little turd
Una caccola

Shit
La merda

Diarrhea
La cacarella

There's nothing like a good **crap**.
*Non c'è niente come una bella **cagata**.*

I'm **constipated.**
*Sono **stitico/a.***

What a stink!
Che puzzo!

In the old days, public toilets were nothing more than a drain hole in the middle of a generally filthy tiled room, often without a door. *Che puzzo!* (What a stink!) These days, most public restrooms have a standard toilet so you don't need to get your fingers all germy. In case they need to drop the kids off at the pool, Italians on the go keep some extra change handy to plug into the turnstile at the public restrooms found in bus and train terminals. (McDonald's is also a great pit stop).

Bathroom
Il bagno

Bidet
Il bidè

Commode
La latrina

Crapper
Il cesso

Pisser
Il pisciatoio

Shitter
Il gabinetto

John
La toilette

Toilet seat
Il trono (throne)

Urinal
Il vespasiano

Other bodily functions
Le altre funzioni corporei

Just **burp** it out.
*Fatti un bel **rutto**.*

I've got the **hiccups**.
*Ho il **singhiozzo**.*

A fart
Una scoreggia
It's no wonder they call those loud motorcycles *scorreggioni* (big farts).

Who's the nasty-ass that **farted**?
*Quale di voi bestie **ha scoreggiato**?*

Who ripped one?
Chi ha fatto quel peto?

It wasn't me who **cut the cheese**.
*Non ero io a **fare quel puzzo**.*
Literally, "made a stink."

Ladies don't fart, they **poot**.
*Le donne non scoreggiano, **fanno aria**.*
Literally, "make air."

You have **bad breath**!
*Ha **l'alito pesante**!*

You smell like a **goat** after three days in the sun.
***Puzzi** come una **capra** dopo tre giorni al sole.*

That's a helluva....
Mamma, che....

> **pimple**
> *brufolo*
>
> **black head**
> *punto nero*
>
> **zit**
> *puntina*

I don't feel so good
Mi sento male

Italy is a hypochondriac's heaven. If you're looking for attention in Italy, nothing works better than playing the old sick card. Italians, in addition to blaming a lot on the *fegato* (liver), are also obsessed with *la digestione* (digestion) and making sure they don't catch *un colpo d'aria* (a draft). Italians will never:

Go swimming for at least two hours after eating. This could seriously *bloccare la digestione* (block your digestion). An ill-timed cappuccino (especially after a meal) can also affect your digestion.

Open a window in a train, or anywhere. *Un colpo d'aria* might somehow manage to seep in and cause countless problems including chills, stiff necks, and sore backs.

Get caught in the rain without an *ombrello* (umbrella). God forbid you should get your hair wet—it could lead to any number of illnesses, including *la cervicale* (cervical arthrosis), a particularly common ailment in Italy whose symptoms include nausea, neck stiffness, and a headache.

Are you all right?
Va tutto bene?

Are you **sick**?
*Stai **male**?*

Call a **doctor!**
*Chiama il **medico**!*

Get me an **aspirin.**
*Dammi un'**aspirina.***

I can't **work** today.
*Non posso **lavorare** oggi.*

I have my **period.**
*Mi sono venute le **mestruazioni**.*

I'm **on the rag**.
*Ho le **mie cose**.*
Literally, "I have my thing."

I've got a **bad liver**.
*Ho **mal di fegato**.*

I caught a **draft.**
*Mi sono preso/a un **colpo d'aria.***

I caught a **cold**.
*Ho il **raffredore**.*

I don't feel well.
*Non **mi sento bene**.*

I feel **bad.**
*Mi sento **male.***

I feel like **shit.**
*Sto di **merda.***

I have a **sore throat.**
*Ho **mal di gola.***

I'm **bleeding.**
*Sto perdendo **sangue.***

I feel **itchy.**
*Mi sento il **prurito.***

My **belly** hurts.
*Mi fa male la **pancia.***

The cold gives me **goosebumps.**
*Il freddo mi dà la **pelle d'oca.***

I'm not well today because I have **cervicale.**
*Oggi non sto bene perché ho la **cervicale.***

Cervicale can come from an open car window, a draft, or any other directed ventilation such as from *un ventilatore* (a fan, related to the word *vento,* or wind). There's no English translation, because we don't get hit by *un colpo d'aria.* Instead, we have mental health days, bad hair days, and other culturally relevant maladies.

CHAPTER 5

Nice & Naughty

Buono & Scandaloso

To the Italians, *il sesso* isn't only about pleasure or making babies; it's a cure-all for everything from dry skin to back pain to menstrual cramps. Enjoyment and feeling good are considered vital to maintaining a state of *benessere* (well-being). The following terms are less about love-making and more about the basic, primal urge. Many of these terms are about as unromantic as it comes and if you dare to use them with the wrong person, don't be surprised to find yourself spending the night alone.

Fucking

Lo scopare

I'd like....
Vorrei....
The following terms are all in the infinitive.

to bang
dare dei colpi

to mount
montarti

to penetrate
penetrarti

to screw
chiavarti
Literally, "to key."

to play the trumpet
trombarti

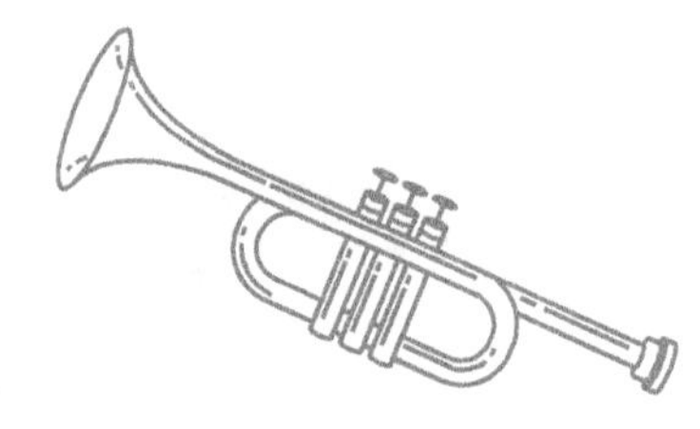

to plow
ararti

to screw
fotterti

to shag
ciularti

Positions
Le posizioni

Italians understand that variety is the spice of life. Although making love is a universal language, there are a couple of Italian terms worth noting. For instance, instead of doing it "doggy-style," the Italians do it *alla pecorina* (sheep-style). *L'amazzone* (the Amazonian) is the term used to describe when a woman sits on a man's face. (It's also called *la pompeiana*, given the position was first depicted on frescoes in Pompei.) Naturally, there are far more variations and regional terms than those listed here.

Do you wanna change positions?
Vuoi voltare il disco?
Literally, "to turn the record over."

What are you in the mood for?
Come ti va?

What's your preference?
Qual è la tua preferenza?

SEXUAL RAPPORT
IL RAPPORTO SESSUALE

The Italian word *scopa* has a bunch of meanings: The Italians love to play a card game called *scopa*, and *una scopa* is a broom; change the noun to masculine, and it becomes *lo scopo* (the goal). *Scopare* is a verb that literally means "to sweep," but in street speak means "to fuck," so next time you sweep the floor—unless it's on all fours—avoid using *scopare* (use *pulire il pavimento*, which means "to clean the floor," instead).

Let's have a **good fuck!**
*Ci vuole una **bella scopata**!*

We fucked a **couple of times**.
*Ci siamo scopati un **paio di volte**.*

Do you wanna **shag** in the car?
*Vuoi **trombare** in macchina?*

I like....
Mi piace....

How 'bout...?
Come va...?

the missionary position
la posizione del missionario

woman on top
la donna sopra

the cowgirl
la smorzacandela
Literally, "the candle snuffer."

sixty-nine
il sessantanove

doggy-style
la posizione alla pecorina
Literally, "sheep style."

through the back door
da dietro

the wheelbarrow
la carriola

a ménage à trois
un ménage à trios

a threesome
un triangolo
Literally, "a triangle."

a blow job
un pompino

The act
L'atto

It's not a race, so *pazienza*. Italians know it's the *viaggio* (journey) that counts, not the destination. By the way, the word *affari* (affairs) generally refers to business ventures. A love affair is referred to as *un'avventura* (an adventure), and a relationship that doesn't necessarily end in marriage is called *una storia* (also the word for "history").

Let's have **an adventure/an affair.**
*Facciamo **un'avventura/una storia.***
In lieu of the verb *avere* (to have), Italian uses the verb *fare* (to do/make) instead.

I'm **excited.**
*Mi sono **eccitato/a.***

Is there somewhere more **private** where we can go?
*C'e una parte più **privata** dove si può stare?*

Do you want to come to **my place**?
*Vuoi venire a **casa mia**?*

Practice **safe sex**!
*Praticate il **sesso sicuro**!*

I practice **free love/polyamory.**
*Sono praticante del **libero amore/poliamore**.*

Our relationship is purely **platonic.**
*Il nostro rapporto è completamente **platonico**.*
You did know this term derives from the Greek philosopher Plato (c. 423–347 BC), didn't you?

Tell me how **you like it.**
*Dimmi come **ti piace**.*

What's your **fantasy**?
*Qual è la tua **fantasia**?*

I'm starving for you!
***Sono allupato/a** per te!*

I'm so **horny** for you!
*Sono proprio **arrapato/a** per te.*

I'm **ready** for you.
*Sono **pronto/a** per te.*

You turn me on!
M'attizzi!

Commands
Pretese

The imperative form of a verb is what you use to tell someone what to do. Get in touch with your bossy side with these expressions.

Kiss me.
Baciami.
From the verb *baciare* (to kiss), and as sweet as a Perugina chocolate *bacio*.

Lick me.
Leccami.
From the verb *leccare* (to lick).

Suck me.
Succhiami.
From the verb *succhiare* (to suck).

Get undressed.
Spogliati.
From the verb *spogliarsi* (to take off your clothes).

Lay down.
Sdraiati.
From the verb *sdraire* (to lay down).

Bend over.
Chinati.
From the verb *chinare* (to bend).

Tell me that you're mine.
Dimmi che sei il mio/la mia.
From the verb *dire* (to say/tell).

Hurry!
Sbrigati!
From the verb *sbrigare* (to hurry).

KISSING
IL BACIARE

Ever loyal to their *madrelingua* (native tongue), instead of French kissing, Italians simply *baciare con la lingua* (to kiss with the tongue).

We French kissed.
Ci siamo baciati con la lingua.

Come on, give me a **kiss**!
*Dai, dammi un **bacio**!*

Did you make-out?
Ci sei andato/a?

Did you go **all the way**?
*Ma, ci sei **andato andato**?*

Who gave you that **ugly hickey**?
*Chi ti ha dato quel **brutto succhiotto**?*

Go slow.
Va piano piano.
From the verb *andare* (to go).

Come on, touch it!
Dai, tocca ferro!
From the verbs *dare* (to give) and *toccare* (to touch).

Give it to me.
Dammelo.
From the verb *dare* (to give) and a wonderful example of a double object pronoun.

Don't stop!
Non smettere!
From the verb *smettere* (to quit).

Hurry up!
Facciamo presto!

It could be between *amanti* or a chance encounter; in either case, *una sveltina* generally does not require getting undressed (beyond what's necessary). And don't expect to cuddle afterward.

We had a **quickie** in between appointments.
*Ci siamo fatti una **sveltina** tra gli appuntamenti.*
You can also use the Americanized version, *un quiko.*

We had **a nooner** during lunch break.
*Abbiamo fatto **una scopatina** durante l'ora di pranzo.*
Scopatina can also be used for "quickie."

We don't have much time. **Let's make it fast.**
*Non abbiamo molto tempo. **Facciamo una cosina veloce**.*
Literally, "to have a fast little thing."

Let's do it **in the car**.
*Facciamo il sesso **a quattro ruote**.*
For the Italians, *il sesso a quattro ruote* (sex on four wheels) is like spaghetti, soccer, and good wine, especially since the invention of the adjustable seat.

We schtuped in the car. My back aches!
Abbiamo fatto una trombata *in macchina. Mi fa male la schiena!*

Penis love
L'Amore del pene

Visit any museum and you'll see lots of images of ancient Romans in ardent appreciation of their maleness. The frescoes preserved in Pompeii and other Roman hot spots are proof that the love affair Italian men have with their sausages ain't nothin' new. The Latin phrase *Hic Habitat Felicitas* said it all: Here Lies Happiness.

Dick
Cazzo

Tireless cock
Spada instancabile

Willy
Pipì

Member
Membro

Donkey dick
Superdotato
Otherwise known as well-endowed.

Schlong
Minchia
Although it has come to singularly mean "dick," this Sicilian term for penis derives from the Latin *mentula*, meaning "stalk" or "tail." It's heard mostly in southern dialects including Calabrese, Barese, and Sicilian. *Minchia* is also used to say "Fuck!" or "Shit!" Also used as an expression of disbelief.

Phallus
Fallo

LOLLIPOP-LOLLIPOP
LECCA-LECCA

When it comes to describing everyone's favorite body parts, Italian and English have more than a few words in common. *Banana* (banana), *carota* (carrot), and *spada* (sword) are all used to describe dicks. Likewise, the Italian words for *caverna* (cavern), *pelo* (fur), and *Giovannina* (Ginny) all describe pussy.

On the other hand, it can be confusing when both languages utilize the same word to describe different things. Take the word *susina* (plum): While in English it can refer to a man's testicle, in Italian it can also mean a pussy. In English, the word "cookie" can also infer a woman's "meow-meow," but in Italian the word *biscotto* describes a man's Johnson.

banana
banana
Or *ciquita*, like the brand name.

twinky
biscotto

chode
fava
Literally, "fava bean."

sausage
salsiccia

pisser
pisello
Literally, "pea."

prick
cactus
Like the prickly desert plant.

wang
asparago
Literally, "asparagus."

winkle
pisellino
Literally, "little pea."

Foreskin
Il prepuzio

Hood
Cappuccio
In slang, this is also used to refer to a condom, but you would ask for un *preservativo* when at the *farmacia* (pharmacy).

He has a beautiful, big, thick one.
Ce l'ha bello, grande, grosso.

His flag is at **half-mast.**
*Ha la bandiera a **mezz'asta**.*

Do you know where I can score some Viagra?
Sa dove posso trovare il Viagra?

Are you familiar with the expression....?
Sei familiare con l'espressione...?

dip the stick
inzuppare il biscotto
Literally, "to dip the cookie."

play the skin flute
suonare il flauto a pelle

put the horse in the stable
mettere il cavallo nella stalla

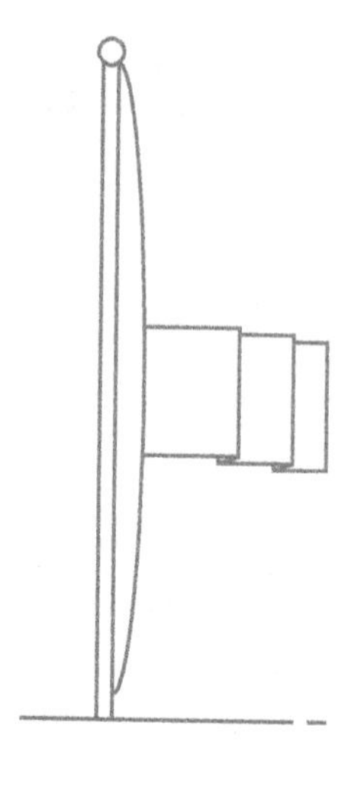

What a...dick.
Che cazzo....

small/tiny
piccolo/piccolissimo

big/huge
grande/grandissimo

hard
duro

flacid
flaccido

long/really long
lungo/lunghissimo

thick/really thick
grosso/grossissimo

I have/he has....
Ho/ha....

a hard-on
un cazzo duro

a boner
un cazzo dritto
Literally, "a straight dick."

I've got a **woody**.
*Sono a **mezzogiorno**.*
Literally, "I'm at noon."

The arrival
L'arrivo

Ejaculation
L'eiaculazione

Sperm
Lo sperma

Cum
La sborra

Cream
La panna

Jizz
Il brodo

To blow your wad
Spegnere la candela
Literally, "to blow out the candle."

I'm about **to come**!
*Sto per **venire**!*

I'm coming!
Vengo!; Arrivo!

That's the spot.
Così va bene.

He was so excited, he **blew his load**.
*Era così eccitato, che si **è bagnato addosso**.*

I exploded with pleasure.
Sono scoppiato/a *dal piacere.*

Sweet dreams!
Sogni d'oro!

You can go away now.
Ora, puoi andare via.

Jewels
I gioielli

The English anatomical term "testicles" comes from the Latin *testiculi*, meaning "witnesses." Back in the day, a man swore an oath on what he held most precious—his family jewels—and that, *signore* and *signori*, is where we get the word *testimonianza* meaning "testimony." I swear!

Balls
Le palle; i coglioni

Ballsack
I broccoli
Like the vegetable.

BALL BUSTING
ROMPERE LE PALLE

to be sick and tired of something
avere le palle piene
Literally, "to have full balls."

to bust balls; to work hard
farsi due palle così
Literally meaning "to do it with two full balls," referring to the fact that someone working very hard is unlikely having a lot of pleasure.

to break someone's balls
rompere i coglioni/le palle

Family jewels
I gioielli di famiglia

Berries
Le caramelle
Literally, "candies."

Nuts
Le castagne
Literally, "chestnuts."

Nads
Le scatole
Literally, "boxes."

Female parts
Le parti femminili

No matter what you call it—girlie parts, box, vajayjay, pussy—you may find it interesting to know that the word "vagina" is Latin for "scabbard" or "sword sheath." Note that to sweeten up a term, Italians insert *bella: Che bella fica!* (What a nice pussy!) *Che bella gnocca!* (What a pretty little cunt!) *Che bella topa!* (What a nice little beaver!)

Vagina
La vagina

Coochie
La fischia
Literally, "whistle."

Cunt
La fregna
Very offensive.

Bell
La campana

Box
La scatola

Gina
La Giovannina
It's kind of a sweet term, when you think about it!

Hole
Il buco
This was originally used in the Napoletan dialect and is very vulgar! Also refers to the other hole.

Guitar
La chitarra

Little mouth
Lo sticchio
Sicilian, the feminine equivalent to the word *minchia* and is wash-your-mouth-out-with-soap material.

Bucket
Il secchio

Thang
La cosa
Also, *quella cosa* (that thing).

Bush
Il cespuglio

Muff
Il triangolino peloso
Literally, "the hairy little triangle."

Minge
La mussa

Snatch
La nassa
Literally, "net."

CREATURES
LE CREATURE

In case you'd like to liken your ladyparts to your favorite animal:

bearded clam
la lumaca
Literally, "snail."

bird
la quaglia
Literally, "quail."

butterfly
la farfalla; la farfallina (the little butterfly)

conch
la conchiglia
This is the same word as the shell-shaped Italian pasta.

nest
il nido

nymph
la ninfa

cooter
la passera; la passerina
Literally, "sparrow" and "little sparrow."

beaver
la topa
Literally, "little mouse." This is heard a lot in the Tuscany area; *sorca*, also meaning "mouse," is also sometimes used to indicate someone that's really hot, as in *Sei proprio una sorcia* (You're really hot!).

Slit
La fessa
Very vulgar!

Clit
Il grilletto

Button
Il bottone

To do cunnilingus
Fare il cunnilingus

To eat pussy
Mangiare la micia

To reach orgasm
Raggiungere l'orgasmo

To stimulate the G-spot
Stimolare il punto G

To titillate with your tongue
Titillare con la lingua

The oldest profession in the world
Il mestiere più antico del mondo

Le puttane (prostitutes) have never had it easy, but they've been around for as long as there have been lonely men in this world. The Romans even had special coins they used in exchange for sex.

Le cortigiane (the courtesans) were in a different class altogether; in addition to providing affection, they were enlisted as companions and conversationalists. Esteemed for their powers to seduce both *il corpo* (the body) and the mind, today's escorts serve in much the same capacity, although it's doubtful they'll be quoting poetry to you.

To procure services
Procurare servizi

A call girl
Una passeggiatrice
Literally, a "walker."

A courtesan
Una cortigiana

A harlot
Una meretrice

A ho
Una mignotta

A hooker
Una baldracca

A hussy
Una sgualdrina

A pimp
Un pappone

A prostitute
Una prostituta

Prostitution
La prostituzione

Sex for hire
Sessinvendola

A slut
Una troia

A streetwalker
Una figlia del marciapiede
Literally, "a daughter of the sidewalk."

A tramp
Una bagascia

A whore
Una puttana

Gigolos
I gigolò

Toyboys, gigolos...the insults are not limited to girls gone wild. Here are a few monikers used to describe male players in the great game of love.

A prodigal son
Un figliol prodigo

A son of a ho
Un figlio di mignotta

A son of a bitch
Un figlio di puttana

A son of a gun
Figlio di buona donna
Euphemism for *figlio di puttana.*

A loser
Un figlio di nessuno
Literally, "a child of no one."

Make love, not war
Fate l'amore, non la guerra

Love is love, and in Italy, love is an art form. Nothing like *una coccolata* (a cuddle) to warm up on a cold night.

Do you want to...?
Vuoi...?

cuddle each other
coccolarci

fondle each other
palpeggiarci

have sex
fare il sesso

hold each other
abbracciarci

make love with me
fare l'amore con me

snuggle each other
rannicchiarci

spoon
fare il cucchiaio

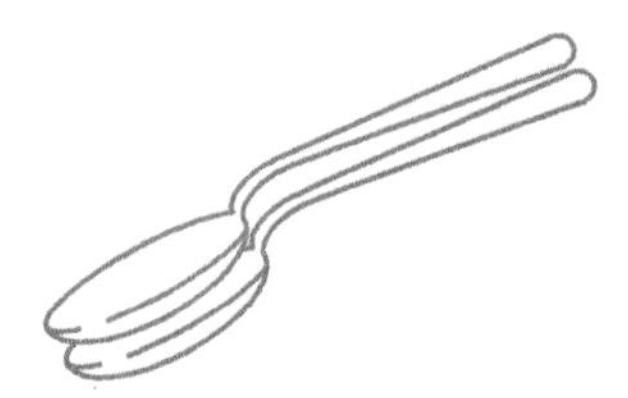

Masturbation
Masturbazione

Your Italian sex-ed teacher might have used the clinical term *masturbazione*, but you'll also hear *autoerotismo*. Whatever you call it, the Italians are no strangers to double-clicking the mouse or beating the one-eyed monster.

Play the pipe
farsi una pipa

Jerk off
farsi una sega
Literally, "to do the saw."

To masturbate
masturbarsi

To spank the monkey
scuotere l'arnese
Literally, "jiggle the tool."

To take care of myself
arrangiarmi da solo

To touch myself
toccarmi

Yo, casanova
Ciao, casanova

"What is life, without love?" asked the Venetian adventurer Giacomo Girolamo Casanova in his memoir that described, in copious detail, his sexual conquests (122 recorded). Unable to keep his *impulsi* under control, he was often on the run in order to avoid going back to *carcere* (jail, related to the word "incarcerate"), a place he had spent considerable time. Not surprisingly, he is one of the first reported to use "assurance caps" (earlier forms of condoms) to prevent both syphilis and pregnancy, although it's doubtful he avoided either.

He is....
Lui è....

a dick
una pirla
Literally, "a pearl." This is a sarcastic term, given *una pirla* usually refers to someone of exceptional quality.

a brown-noser
un lecchino
Literally, "a little licker."

an impotent
un impotente

a limp dick
un rammolito

like a newbie
come una eiaculazione precoce
Literally, "a premature ejaculation."

a show-off
uno sborrone

a sissy
una femminuccia

a voyeur
un guardone

a well-endowed man
un ben dotato

How's it goin', tiger?
Come va, tigre?

It's not what, but how, something is said. *La mia zozzona* (my little tramp) can be quite a turn-on if you're both *nudi* (naked).

It's another story if, on the other hand, she's the *sudiciona* (nasty bitch) that left you for your best friend.

You are such....
Sei proprio....

a tiger in bed
una tigre del materasso
Literally, "a tiger of the mattress."

a great piece of pussy
una bella gnocca

a nice ride
una bella bicicletta
Literally, "a beautiful bicycle."

a sex pot
una donnina allegra
Literally, "a happy woman."

a sexual mentor
una nave scuola
This term, meaning "school ship," tends to be used to describe when an older, more experienced woman teaches the ropes to a younger man.

a dirty bitch
una sporcacciona

a nasty bitch
una sudiciona

a cocksucker
una bocchinara

a tramp
una zozza

a prude
una morigerata

Contraception
Contraccettivi

The word "venereal" (as in, disease) derives from the love goddess Venus. Use an *impermeabile* (raincoat)! They come in all shapes, sizes, and *colori*. You can buy birth control at any *farmacia*, and you can often find condoms in vending machines outside clubs. Better safe than sorry.

Do you have...?
Hai...?

a condom
un preservativo
This word is not to be used to describe "preservatives," like all that crap they use in our food to make it last until the next millennium. In that case, Italian uses the word *conservanti*.

a balloon
un palloncino

pajamas
un pigiamino

a parachute
un paracadute

a Trojan
un goldone
Because the wrapper used to be gold.

lubricant
il lubrificante

You use **birth control**, right?
*Usi **l'anticoncezionale**, vero?*

You better put on a **raincoat**.
*Devi metterti un **impermeabile**.*

Use a **glove**.
*Usa un **guanto**.*

Did you bring **protection**?
*Hai portato la **protezione**?*

I brought a **condom.**
*Ho portato un **profilattico**.*

I'm on the **pill**.
*Prendo la **pillola**.*

I use an **IUD**.
*Uso la **spirale**.*

I use a **diaphragm**.
*Uso il **diaframma**.*

Have you been **tested** for AIDS?
*Hai mai fatto le **analisi** per l'AIDS?*

Have you ever had an **STI**?
*Hai mai avuto una **malattia venerea**?*

Sorry to ask, but you don't have **herpes, syphilis, or hepatitis C**, do you?
*Mi dispiace chiederti, ma non hai **l'herpes, la sifilide, o l'epatite C**, vero?*

Transgressions
Trasgressioni

Rome's history is filled with images and writings depicting a cornucopia of sex, *sadismo*, and madness. Dressed in leather harnesses with metal studs, gladiators were notorious for their rugged, bad-ass sex appeal in a libidinous public hungry for action. Role-play and power games were a big turn-on for a percentage of promiscuous Romans, and their graffiti, poetry, and *arte* were filled with pornographic depictions of raw, unashamed copulation, not to mention *dominazione* and *sottomissione*. This is another reason Pompeii was such a popular destination before Vesuvius covered the ancient spa city in lava.

Bondage and discipline
Il bondage e la disciplina
Also abbreviated to B&D.

Swinger party
Lo scambio di coppia
Literally, "couple exchange."

Domination and submission
La dominazione e la sottomissione
Also abbreviated to D&S or DS.

Eroticism
L'erotismo

Fetishism
Il feticismo

Orgy
L'ammucchiata
Literally, "pile."

Safe, sound, and consensual
Sicuro, sano, e consensuale

Safeword
Parola di sicurezza

I'm your slave boy.
Sono il tuo ***schiavo****.*

CHAPTER 6

Smack Talk

Le Parole Pettegolose

Italians are hyperbolic people. They can be the kindest, most *gentile* (nice) people on the planet, but they can also be vicious, hypocritical gossips. So if you want to be like an Italian, along with learning to pander and oblige, you're going to have to learn how to swear. Gear up with a few insults and *minacce* (threats).

Pissed off

Incazzato

I'm **fed up** with this shit!
Mi sono stufato/a *con questa merda!*

I've had it up to here!
Ho le palle piene!
Literally, "My balls are full."

I'm really **ticked off**.
Sono veramente ***incavolato/a***.

You're gettin' on my nerves.
Mi fai venire il nervoso.

Don't piss me off.
Non mi scazzare.

Okay, now I'm pissed!
Adesso sono incazzato/a.

What are you ranting about?
Ma di cosa stai delirando?

I'm completely **infuriated.**
Sono proprio ***arrabbiato/a.***

Be careful, **shithead**!
Sta' attento ***testa di merda!***

Lighten up!
Rilassati!

Get off my case!
Lasciami in pace!
Literally, "Leave me in peace!"

That poor bastard was so **raging mad** when he found his wife screwing his son's best friend.
Si è ***incazzato nero*** *quando ha trovato la moglie a scopare l'amichetto di suo figlio.*
The word *nero* literally means "black."

You talkin' to me?
Stai parlando a me?

When an Italian gets sick 'n' tired of being sick 'n' tired, all bets are off.

What's your fuckin' issue?
Mah, che cazzo hai?

You gotta problem with me?
Ce l'hai con me?

I'll get you for that!
Questa me la paghi!

Don't bother me.
Non disturbarmi.

What the fuck do you mean by that?
Che cazzo intendi?

What the fuck do you want?
Che cazzo vuoi?

What'd you say? You wanna repeat that?
Che cosa hai detto? Lo vuoi ripetere?

Have you gone mad?
Sei divento/a matto/a?

Now you're goin' too far.
Adesso stai esagerando.

It's none of your damn business!
Che te ne frega!

Get out of here!
Vattene!

Go take a shit!
Va' a cagare!

Go to hell!
Va' all'inferno!

FUCK OFF!
VAFFANCULO!

If you have to choose one insult, make it *Vaffanculo!* (In some dialects, you will hear the "c" pronounced like a "g.")

Literally meaning "go do it in the ass," it can be employed when you spill *caffé* on your *camicia bianca* (white shirt) or discover your car has *una gomma a terra* (a flat). There's the *Vaffanculo!* you scream at your *stronzo* (turd) of a boss the day you get canned, probably for swearing too much. And there's the final *Vaffanculo!* you might utilize when you give your lying, cheating *amante* (lover) the kick in the ass he or she deserves. This particular version was even made into a national campaign *Vaffa-Day* (or "V-day") by the popular comedian and social activist Beppe Grillo to protest government corruption.

I hate you!
Ti odio!

Suck me.
Ciucciami!

Go away!
Vai via!

Get outta here!
Vattene!

Disappear!
Sparisci!

Motherfucker!
Porca puttana!

Shitface!
Faccia di merda!

Mind your own beeswax!
Fatti i fatti tuoi!
Literally, "Mind your own facts."

Gossip
Sparlare

Unleash the catty bitch inside of you and smack around these nasty little *commenti*. Of course we all know your *merda* don't stink, though.

I don't like **to gossip**, but who does she think she is?
Non mi piace ***fare il pettegolo*** *ma chi pensa di essere?*

Scandolous!
Scandaloso!

Is he gay?
È gay?

I hope so/not.
Spero di sì/no.

I heard he has sex with men and with women.
Ho sentito che ha rapporti sessuali con uomini e con donne.

Do you wanna hear **a rumor**?
Vuoi sentire ***un pettegolezzo****?*

Quit talking **nonsense**.
Non dire delle ***sciocchezze****.*

She thinks she's all that.
Se la tira quella.

It's enough to mention his name and she cries.
Basta pronunciare il suo nome e piange.

Don't be such a **gossip**.
Non essere ***un/a pettegolo/a****.*

Fightin' words
Parole di lotta

Let's face it, Italians are lovers, not fighters. Rarely do you see a group of drunk Italians getting into a brawl. *Can che abbaia non morde.* (The dog that barks doesn't bite.) They'll curse and stomp their feet until they're blue in the face, but in the end they're all talk. Now, Italian *nonne* (grandmothers) are another story. You're definitely asking for a smack across the face if you piss them off.

Even if Italians aren't big on fighting, they're good at dishing it out. There's a certain poetry to Italian threats. They don't just say, "Hey, I'm going to hit you." Instead, expect to hear things like:

If you don't close your mouth, **I'll split your head open.**
Se non chiudi la bocca, ***ti spacco la testa****.*

You truly have the face of an ass.
Hai proprio una faccia da culo.

I'm counting down from three. If at two you don't shut the fuck up, at one I'm gonna hurt you.
Conto fino a tre. Se al due non ti zitti, all'uno ti gonfio.

Can you smell **the stink** from the bullshit that comes out of your mouth?
Ma la senti ***la puzza*** *delle stronzate che dici?*

If my dog had your face, I'd shave its ass and teach it to walk backward!
Se il mio cane avesse la tua faccia, gli raderei il culo e gli insegnerei a camminare al contrario!

Shit into your hand and **slap yourself**.
Cacati in mano e ***pigliati a schiaffi****.*

Your bad breath is so gross that you kill flies midair.
Il tuo alito è talmente schifoso che ammazzi le mosche al volo.

You're so stupid, your last neuron died of loneliness.
Sei così stupido che il tuo ultimo neurone è morto di solitudine.

You're such a **ball breaker**, you'd need two of you to make one dickhead!
Sei così ***coglione*** *che ce ne vogliono due come te per fare una testa di cazzo!*

You're such a turd, your mother shit you out.
Sei così stronzo che tua madre ti ha cagato.

All of these terms are used interchangeably by Italians to indicate their disbelief when hearing someone's bullshit story.

What a load of crap!
Che cazzata!

What...!
Che...!

shit
puttanata
From *puttana*, the word for "whore."

bull
troiata
From *troia*, the word for "slut."

bullshit
stronzata
From *stronzo*, the word for "turd."

crap
cagata

garbage
cavolata
Literally, "cabbage."

Punches and kicks
Pugni e calci

I'm gonna hit you so bad, you'll go back in time!
Ti dò una sberla *che ti mando indietro nel tempo!*

I'll hurt you so bad that I'll get out of prison before you get out of the hospital.
Ti farò talmente male *che uscirò prima io di galera che tu dall'ospedale.*

I'll kick your ass so hard, your teeth will shatter.
Ti tiro un calcio in culo *così forte che ti spacco i denti.*

Be careful before I give you....
Stai attento che ti dò....

a smack
una sberla

a slap
uno schiaffo

a hit
una botta

a kick in the ass
un calcio in culo

If you try it with me, **I'll deck you**!
*Se ci provi, **ti tiro un ceffone**!*

Does your mommy know you'll be spending the night in the **hospital?**
*Lo sa tua mamma che stanotte dormi all'**ospedale**?*

I'll break your legs.
***Ti spezzo** le gambe.*

Do you really want to spend tomorrow shitting the teeth I made you swallow?
Domani vuoi passare una giornata cagando i denti che ti ho fatto ingoiare?

I'll rip your arms off and hit you with them!
***Ti strappo le braccia** e te le tiro addosso.*

Don't make me **bitchslap you**!
*Non farti **dare uno schiaffone**!*

I'll grab you, break you, eat you, and shit you out right here!
Te prendo, te spezzo, te mangio, e te cago qua intorno!

Insults
Sgarbi

Using only one insult would be like eating the same kind of pasta every day—it's better to have *varietà*.

Don't act like a **dumbass.**
*Non comportarti da **sciocco**.*

You know, you're a real **fool**.
*Sei proprio **scemo**, sai?*

He/She is a **moron**.
*Lui/Lei è un/a **cretino/a**.*

What a **dummy**—he doesn't understand dick.
*Che **balordo**—lui non capisce un cazzo.*

That **punk** cheated me outta five bucks.
*Quell'**imbroglione** mi ha fregato cinque dollari.*

WHAT A DRAG!
CHE PALLE!

Che palle! (literally, "what balls!") is among the most commonly muttered slang in the Italian language. Italians who like to pretend they're above swearing may also use the term *Che pizza!* (What pizza!). *Che palle* is used to say "What bullshit!" as well as to express boredom, annoyance, and impatience in a variety of *situazioni* such as:

- When the bottom of a soggy paper bag drops out and all the garbage with it...*Che palle!*
- Your *professore* gives you a pop quiz...*Che palle!*
- Your girlfriend rags on you for not calling...*Che palle!*

Ugh, what a **bore.**
Uffa, che ***noia****.*

Use your turn signals, you **piece of shit**!
Usa le frecce, ***pezzo di merda****!*
Cut off? Tell him off! And if the driver can't hear you, you can always give him your middle finger (an international gesture that needs no translation). When he runs your car off the road and into a ditch, you can always use your thumb to *fare autostop* (hitchhike).

Dumbass driving, peril thriving.
Deficiente *al volante, pericolo costante.*
The Italian rhymes too, if you didn't already notice.

You're better off on a **donkey**.
*Ti conviene tornare sull'****asino****.*

You drive like a deaf old lady who forgot her glasses and has the shakes.
Guidi come una vecchietta senza occhiali, sorda e tremolante.

He/She is....
Lui/Lei è....

You're acting like....
Ti comporti come....

a pain in the ass
un/a rompicoglioni
Literally, "a ball-breaker."

a rude motherfucker
un/a maleducato/a

a son of a bitch
un figlio di puttana

a turd
uno/a stronzo/a
This versatile word can simultaneously mean "dumbass," "schmuck," "jerk," and "ass-wipe," depending on the user and how it's used.

a bastard
un bastardo

a brownnoser
un leccapiedi
Literally, "a foot licker."

an oaf
un cafone

a slob
uno sporcaccione
Literally, "a big pig."

a chump
un/a burino/a

a fake
un'impostore

a poser
un pagliaccio
Literally, "a clown."

a jokester
un/a birichino/a
A *birichinata* is a practical joke.

a cocksucker
un/a bocchinaro/a

a pervert
un/a porco/a
Literally, "pig."

What a bitch
Che cagna

She might be your (ex-) best friend, after you've discovered she's a lying whore who dissed you the whole time she pretended to be your bestie. Or, she could be the stranger that cut you off during *l'ora di punta* (rush hour).

What a....
Che....

She is a major....
Lei è un/una proprio....

biotch
troietta
From the word *troia.*

bitch-ass
disgraziata

cocktease
puttanella
Derivative of the word *puttana.*

heifer
vacca

ugly-ass chick
pugno nell'occhio
Literally, "a punch in the eye."

hag
marmitta
Literally, "a marmot."

prude
morigerata

dog
cammello
Literally, "a camel," and used to refer to a very unattractive woman.

YOUR MAMA AND SISTER...
TUA MAMMA E SORELLA...

This is where the real Italian comes out. Insulting someone's mother or sister is a shortcut to hell.

Your mama/sister is...
Tua mamma/sorella è...

so ugly, she makes onions cry.
così brutta che fa piangere le cipolle.

so stupid that whenever she goes to the bar she shits herself because the door says PUSH.
così stupida che davanti alla porta del bar si caga sempre addosso perché c'è scritto SPINGERE.

so scary that Parliament officially changed Halloween to her birthday.
così spaventosa che il Parlamento ha ufficialmente spostato Halloween al giorno del suo compleanno.

gives blow jobs to dead dogs.
una che fa le pompe ai cani morti.

So how's your mother and my children?
Come sta tua moglie e i miei figli?

sneaky motherfucker
furbacchiona
From the word *furbo/a* (sly); *la furbizia* refers to "slyness."

witch
strega

Loserville
Sfigati

This section is for your boss, your husband, your boyfriend, your lover. He's the *bastardo* that cheated on you. He's the *briccone* (asshole) standing next to you at the DMV, the *stronzetto* (dipshit) who tried to rip you off, the *figlio di puttana* (son of a bitch) who ate the last chocolate.

He's such a/an...!
Lui è un vero...!

I can't believe I ever slept with that...!
Com'è possibile ho dormito con quel...!

asshole
briccone

asswipe
lecchino

cocklicker
leccacazzi

cocksucker
pompinaio

dickhead
minchione

dicksucker
succhiatore

dipshit
stronzetto

idiot
idiota

pathetic loser
sciagurato/a

rascal
mascalzone

schmuck
cornuto

sucker
gonzo

tramp
barbone

You're a real Einstein!
Hai scoperto l'America!
Literally, "You discovered America!" This is a sarcastic statement, Einstein!

What the dick...?
Che cazzo...?

Cazzo! This catch-all swear word translates to cock, dick, or prick, but its usage extends far beyond anatomy 101. This five-letter word is used every-fuckin'-where, in the same way that "fuck" is used in English as an adjective, like "fucking bastard," or as a verb, like "Fuck you!," and as a noun, like "a fuck."

Now, if you're not comfortable with using the word because you don't speak Italian yet, I suggest you substitute it one of many euphemisms used instead: *cavolo* (cabbage), *cacchio*, and *Kaiser*. Go ahead, say *Che cavolo!* (What the cabbage!). It's like saying, "What the fudge!"

You're a real....
Sei proprio un....

dick
cazzo

big dick
cazzone
This is also used to describe a poser.

dickhead
testa di cazzo

Fuck yeah!
Cazzuto!

He could give a goddamn about her.
Non gliene importa un cazzo di lei.

He doesn't do dick.
Non fa un cazzo.

How the fuck should I know?
Che cazzo ne so!

Holy fuck!
Cazzo di Budda!
Literally, "Buddha's dick."

It's not worth a rat's ass.
Non vale un cazzo.

I could give a flying fuck.
Non me ne frega un cazzo.

Mind your own fucking business.
Fatti i cazzi tuoi!

My ass!
Col cazzo che!
Used sarcastically to contradict something someone has said.

Quit busting my chops.
Non mi rompere il cazzo.
Literally, "breaking my dick."

That sucks.
Sono cazzi.
Literally, "They're dicks."

When hell freezes over.
Quando il cazzo fa l'unghia.
Literally, "When a dick turns into a finger."

You're bugging the shit out of me.
Mi stai sul cazzo.

He who sleeps with dogs, wakes up with fleas

Chi va a letto con i cani, si leva con le pulci

While not officially swearing, the following terms are all used to describe those deemed unworthy (which includes just about everyone that isn't *famiglia*). These will be especially helpful the next time you get punked by someone. You might remember hearing your *nonna* use these terms to describe any number of people, including politicians, your uncle, your neighbor, or anyone that has disappointed her.

To bully
bullizzare

A criminal
Un criminale

A crook
Un ladrone

A delinquent
Un delinquente

A hustler
Un furbone

A lowlife
Un poco di buono

A gangsta
Un mafioso

An outlaw
Un fuorilegge

A petty thief
Un ladruncolo

A scumbag
Una carogna

A thief
Un ladro

A thug
Una teppista

A troublemaker
Un malvivente

A villain
Un villano

A wrongdoer
Un malfattore

Liar, liar!
Bugiardo, bugiardo!

Italians give a lot of *importanza* to a person's word. Listen to just about any opera and you'll hear someone crying *Bugiardo!* (Liar!), which can also mean "Fraud!" or "Phony!" There are a few words used to describe people whose opinions of themselves may be a bit *esagerato*, or exaggerated, but as a double entendre (which in French means double meaning, stupid), it can also mean "burned out."

A liar
Un/a bugiardo/a

A fraud
Una truffa

A bullshitter
Una ballista

A braggart
Un fanfarone

A braggadocio
Uno smargiasso

A blowhard
Un gradasso

A show-off
Un millantatore

A bullshit artist
Uno sbruffone

A roughneck
Uno spaccone

My God!
Dio mio!

Consider this book a manual on what *not* to say in church! As one might expect from a country with *una chiesa* (a church) on every corner, Italian employs quite a few colorful blasphemies that could almost sound like *preghiere* (prayers)—*Oh Dio buono!*—except you're no priest, and this is hardly a religious *esperienza.*

Although rarely enforced, it is actually a bona fide offense to *bestemmiare* (curse) in public. Aside from its moral *implicazioni* (implications), in Italy, taking the Lord's name in vain will get you more than a spaghetti lashing and could result in a misdemeanor charge.

By Jove.
Per Giove.

Bloody Christ!
Mannaggia Cristo!

Christ!
Cristo!

Criminy!
Cribbio!
A euphemism for Cristo.

Devil!
Diavolo!

Beast God!
Dio bestia!
Very offensive.

CURSED
MALEDETTO

The adjectives *maledetto/a* (cursed) and *dannato/a* (damned) can be used to exaggerate any situation, like "I'm crazy starving." (Or, if you live on the West Coast, "I'm hella starving.")

I'm **hella starving.**
Ho una ***fame maledetta.***

Quit with that **goddamn music**!
Smetti con quella ***maledetta musica!***

I was **fucking freezing.**
Avevo un ***freddo maledetto.***

I was **fucking scared shitless.**
Avevo una ***paura maledetta.***

Where'd that ***damned dog*** go?
Dov'è finito quel ***dannato cane****?*

Dammit!
Mannaggia!
Used often, but still considered vulgar.

Dog God!
Dio cane!

For heaven's sake!
Per carità!

For the love of God.
Per l'amore di Dio.

Go to hell!
Va' all'inferno!

Go to the devil!
Va' al diavolo!

Cursed!
Maledizione!

Jesus!
Gesù!

My God!
Dio mio!

Mother of God!
Madonna!

Pig god!
Porco dio!
Porco dio is exceptionally offensive; euphemisms include *Porco due!* (pig two) and *Porco zio!* (pig uncle). Sometimes the "p" is eliminated to make the expression more palatable; the often-controversial Prime Minister Berlusconi was known to utter *Orco Dio.*

Mary's a pig!
Porca Madonna!

Saint Mary!
Santa Maria!

Shit God!
Dio merda!
Very offensive.

Gosh!
Zio!
A euphemism for *Dio*.

Virgin Mary!
Madonna vergine!

To swear or not to swear
Bestemmiare o non bestemmiare

These verbs and idiomatic expressions related to cussing may come in handy one day when you're just sick 'n' tired of listening to someone's filthy-shit-foul piehole. Just add *non* in front of a verb to tell someone not to do something, as in *Non bestemmiare, testa di cazzo*! (Quit it with the dirty language, dickhead!)

A blaspheme
Una bestemmia

A curse
Una maledizione

A cuss word
Una parolaccia

Quit **cussing**, you ugly, deficient piece of shit.
Non ***maledire****, brutto, deficiente pezzo di merda.*

Quit **swearing**!
Non ***bestemmiare****!*

Nut jobs swear at everyone.
I matti *imprecano contro tutti.*

Chill out

Rilassati

The Italians have a saying, *il vino si fa con l'uva* ("wine is made from grapes"). Obviously, you've got to stomp on a lot of grapes to get the juice to make the wine. After all the arm waving and teeth clenching, isn't it time to make nice?

It's not **worth** it.
*Non **vale** la pena.*

Don't get yourself all worked up.
Non esagerare.
Literally, "Don't exaggerate."

Leave it alone.
***Lascialo** stare.*

Let it go.
Lascia perdere.

Don't lose your head.
Non perdere la testa.

Calm down.
***Calma**.*

Can't we agree to **disagree**?
*Possiamo convenire di essere in **disaccordo**?*

Can't we just **get along**?
*Perchè non possiamo **andare d'accordo**?*

Chill!
Tranquillo/a!

For the love of mother, **quit it**!
*Per l'amore di madre, **basta**!*

I can **explain** everything.
*Posso **spiegare** tutto.*

I don't wanna **argue**.
*Non voglio **litigare**.*

It's not what it looks like!
Non è quello che sembra!

It's useless getting all worked up over such **stupidity**.
*È inutile arrabbiarsi per una **stupidaggine**.*

Let's make **nice.**
*Facciamo la **pace**.*
Literally, "Let's make peace."

Make love, not war.
***Fate l'amore**, non la guerra.*

Quit with the **fighting;** let's have a happy ending.
*Basta con questi **litigi;** facciamo finire bene la storia.*
The Italian verb *litigare* (to argue) is related to the English word "litigate."

We're on the same **team**.
*Siamo sulla stessa **squadra**.*

CHAPTER **7**

Pop Culture, Fashion, & Technology

La Cultura Pop, La Moda, & La Tecnologia

Italians practically invented *il divertimento* (amusement), whether you're talking about *teatro* (theater), *musica*, *film*, or *la moda* (fashion). Beyond their *amore* of *arte* and fashion, when Italians are at home they're usually surfing the net and watching bad TV right alongside the rest of us.

Art

L'arte

Don't be a dumb-ass *ignorante*. Take the time to bone up on your art history. Italy hosts some of the most extraordinary artistic expressions the world has ever known; if you didn't even know that the word "Renaissance" means "rebirth," put the book down for a *minuto* and rethink your priorities. Italians enjoy viewing their national treasures. (Besides, there's a lot more to see at the *museo* than just art.) Study up on some Michelangelo and Leonardo so you can spit some facts at the museum-going hotties. *Arte*, anyone?

Wanna check out the **museum**?
*Vuoi andare al **museo**?*

Who's this artist? I like the way he painted those **nudies**.
*Chi è quest'artista? Mi piace come ha dipinto quei **nudi**.*

Isn't the Renaissance the name of a **clothing store**?
*Il Rinasciamento non è il nome di un **negozio di abbigliamento**?*

> No, the store is called Rinascente, **idiot**.
> *No, il negozio si chiama La Rinascente, **idiota**.*

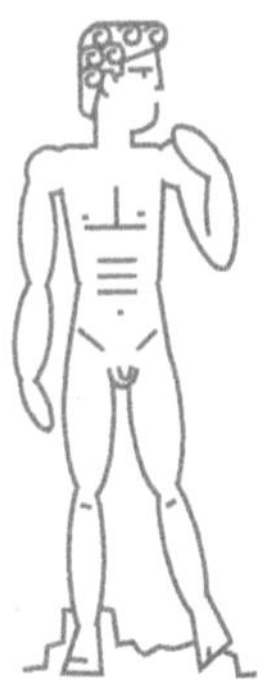

Didn't they drink a lot during the **Baroch**?
*Non bevevano molto durante il **Barocco**?*

Look at the **cute asses** on those **cherubs**!
*Guarda i **culetti** su quei **putti**!*

My dog could **paint it** better than that.
*Il mio cane potrebbe **dipingerlo** meglio.*

What a **teeny weenie** on that statue!
*Che **pisellino** su quella statua!*

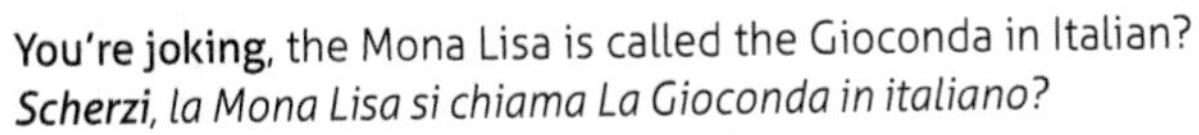

You're joking, the Mona Lisa is called the Gioconda in Italian?
***Scherzi**, la Mona Lisa si chiama La Gioconda in italiano?*

Why is that **painting** all fuzzy?
*Perché quel **quadro** è tutto crespo?*

> That's called **Impressionism**, fool.
> *Si chiama **Impressionismo**, scemo.*

I'm more into **Gothic**. It's all vampiry.
*Mi va più il **Gotico**. È pieno di vampiri.*

Abstract art is too...abstract for me.
***L'Astrattismo** è troppo...astratto per me.*

How come there's **pop art** but no mom art?
*Perché c'è **la pop art** ma non c'è la mamma art?*

Art is that which you can't understand its significance, but you understand it has significance. —Anonymous
Arte è ciò di cui non si capisce il significato, ma si capisce che ha un significato. —Anonimo
A good one to use to impress your sophisticated friends.

One should live their life as though it were a **work of art**.
*Bisogna fare della propria vita come si fa un'**opera d'arte**.*
—Gabriele D'Annunzio

Gabriele knows what he's talking about.

Artwork is always a **confession**.
*L'opera d'arte è sempre una **confessione**. —Umberto Eco*

Music
La musica

When it comes to *musica*, rock still cracks open the skies and brings thousands of concert goers to the old cobblestoned open *piazzas*. Lady Gaga and Sting regularly make the Italian circuit. Italian bands like Zucchero and Paolo Conti still bring in aging rockers. Newer bands include *Il Pan del Diavolo* (The Devil's Bread), *Tre Allegri Ragazzi Morti* (Three Happy Dead Boys), and *Subsonica*. Other popular singers include Gianluca Capozzi, Pino Daniele, Giorgia, Jovanotti, Manuel Aspidi, Elisa, and Fabrizio Moro. Jazz, blues, hip-hop, house, and reggae are all popular too. And of course, Italians still weep for opera.

What kind of **music** do you listen to?
*Che tipo di **musica** ti piace?*

What's the name of that **song**?
*Qual è il nome di quella **canzone**?*

I can't listen to this **crap**!
*Questa **roba** è inascoltabile!*

I'd give anything to see some....
Darei un occhio per vedere....
Literally, "I'd give an eye."

OPERA
L'OPERA

Move over Andrea Boccelli: Hotties like Patrizio Buanne draw scores of fans (and the occasional stalker). Italian opera has as much drama as a daytime soap. The lyricism and cadence of all those open vowels and trilled *r*'s send shivers down the spines of even the tightest, most repressed of souls. Between the divas and prima donnas, the sopranos and the tenors, there's enough love, adultery, treachery, betrayal, and *ossessione* to keep Dante's inferno filled to the brim with sinners, horny noblemen, jilted lovers, and murderers. Add some instrumentals and your mood will be instantly enhanced, without the use of any mind-altering substances.

Opera singers got some pipes on them.
***Le cantanti d'opera** hanno un'ugola d'oro.*

You're acting like a **diva.**
*Ti stai comportando come una **diva.***

We got great seats in the **balcony**.
*Abbiamo acquistato i posti sul **balcone**.*

How much do I owe you for the **tickets**?
*Quanto devo per i **biglietti**?*

Is there an **intermission**? I'm gonna wet myself.
C'e' un intervallo? Sto per pisciarmi addosso.

Let's blast some....
Mettiamo un po' di....a palla.

I'm crazy about....
Impazzisco per....

blues
il blues

classical
la musica classica

hip-hop
l'hip-hop

house
l'house

gospel
la musica gospel

indie
la musica indie

jazz
la musica jazz

karaoke
il karaoke

Latin-American
la latino-americana

pop
la musica pop

punk
la musica punk

R&B
il R e B

reggae
la musica reggae

rock 'n' roll
il rock 'n' roll

techno
la techno

traditional music
la musica tradizionale

God, I **hate** pop punk.
*Dio mio, **odio** il pop punk.*

I love jazz **improvisation**!
*Amo l'**improvvisazione** jazz!*

Jazz is where it's at!
Nient'altro che jazz!

Go back to karaoke!
Torna al karaoke!

Reggae music says we're all one. **It's a beautiful thing**, man.
***La musica reggae** dice che siamo tutti uno.* ***Che bello**, amico.*

How come all **house music** sounds the same?
Come mai tutta la ***musica house è uguale****?*

Is it just Shakira, or are all Latin-American pop **singers** way hot?
Ma è solo Shakira o tutte le ***cantanti*** *latino-americane sono bone?*

Lady Gaga rocked that **concert** like nobody's business.
Lady Gaga ha scatenato il ***concerto*** *come nessun altro.*

The **show** sucked.
Lo ***spettacolo*** *faceva schifo.*

The **sound quality** was so shitty.
La ***qualità della musica*** *faceva proprio cagare.*

Fashion
La moda

Fashion is its own language, and the list of Italian words corresponding to fashion is extensive. You can tell a lot about a person by their shoes, and if you're into people watching (and Italians are great to watch), observe what personal choices communicate, from handbags to briefcases to eyeglasses to the brand of jean someone wears. What *messaggio* are you communicating?

Skinny jeans are **in fashion** this year.
I jeans attillati a sigaretta sono ***di moda*** *quest'anno.*

Big shoulders are definitely **out of fashion**.
Le spalle larghe sono definitivamente ***fuori moda****.*
Or you can use the English word "out."

People dress very well in Italy.
***Si vestono** molto bene in Italia.*

At the party, I sported an **evening dress**.
*Per la festa ho indossato un'**abito da sera**.*

Here, **try this** on.
*Ecco, **prova questo**.*

Do you have a **changing room**?
*Avete un **spogliatoio**?*

What **size** do you wear?
*Che **taglia** porti?*

Regardless of the money he spent, he's still a **bad dresser**.
*Nonostante i soldi che ha speso, è ancora uno **sfattone**.*

You look like a real **redneck** with those shoes.
*Sembri proprio **tamarro** con quelle scarpe.*

Sexy sexy

Sexy sexy

Sexy in Italy seems effortless, as though Italians were born knowing how to dress. Throw on an exquisite neck scarf, add a cashmere twin set, camel-colored cigarette pants, a string of pearls, and you're an Italian woman. Really cool eyewear doesn't hurt—designer glasses are *de rigueur*. And never get between an Italian and his Bulgari watch.

I fit into my **old jeans**!
*Sono rientrata nei **vecchi jeans**!*

Good God, these jeans are **tight**.
*Dio buono, questi jeans sono **strettissimi**.*

Leggings show off your **great bod**!
*I leggings fanno vedere il tuo **fisico mozzafiato**.*

Does **this** look good on me?
*Mi sta bene **questo**?*

Fine!
Togo!
Toghissimo makes it "Damn fine!"

It looks **great** on you!
*Ti sta **benissimo**!*

Out of this world!
*È la fine del **mondo**!*
Literally, "the end of the world."

You're a **knockout**!
*Sei uno **schianto**!*

Way hot!
Super bono/a!

You're as gorgeous as a **model**!
*Sei bella come una **fotomodella**!*

You're looking **great**!
*Hai un aspetto **magnifico**!*

Your **ass** belongs on a statue.
*Hai un **culo** di marmo.*
Literally,"You have a marble ass."

Clothes
I vestiti

I'm looking for....
Cerco....

I'd like to buy....
Vorrei comprare....

a belt
una cintura

a dress
un abito; un vestito

a jacket
una giacca

a sweater
una maglia

jeans
i jeans

a purse
una borsa

leggings
i leggings

lingerie
della lingerie

pants
i pantaloni

A couple of Italian bra shopping tips: Bring the item you plan on wearing with you so that the sales lady can equip you with *il reggiseno giusto* (the correct bra). Trends change all the time. That pumped up decollage so popular a few years ago has now been replaced with a more down-to-earth, less pretentious style in synch with a leaner *economia.*

A...bra.
Un reggiseno....

push-up
push-up

sports
sportivo

balconette
balconcino

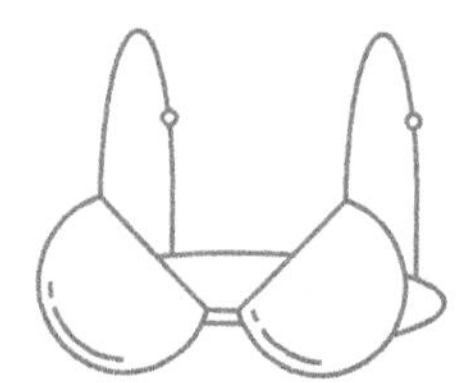

A thong
Un tanga

Underwear
Lo slip

Undies
Le mutandine

This bra is **just right.**
*Questo reggiseno è **giusto giusto**.*

HOW TO UPDATE YOUR LOOK
COME AGGIORNARE IL VOSTRO LOOK

When it comes to expressing themselves, Italians these days are less concerned with how much they own as they are with what they wear. Better to have a high-quality, well-crafted jacket you wear most days than a closet full of cheaply made clothes bought at the discount store. *La qualità* (quality) goes a long way. Here are a few fashion guidelines:

Tip#1: Shoes. Italian ladies still love to wear high-heels when they go out, but if they're walking around town, they're more likely to wear a pair of flats.

Tip#2: Jeans. It's all about the ass. Try on a hundred pairs until you find the ones that cradle your buns like a welcome set of Italian man-hands. Buy three pairs, and then throw out everything that doesn't make you feel like a rockstar the second you slip them on.

Tip#3: Colors. Italians aren't afraid of bright colors. Italian men regularly wear pink or purple. Let out your wild Italian child and put on a color you wouldn't normally wear.

Tip#4: Accessories. Find an *anello* (ring), *braccialetto* (bracelet), or an *orologio* (watch) that you can wear every day. You can never overaccessorize in Italy.

Tip#5: Natural. Go easy on the fake stuff, especially fake tans and artificial nails. There aren't a lot of nail salons in Italy, and Italians do not do French manicures. And no look is complete without a signature scent.

Your tits look **gigantic**.
*Le tue tette sono **gigantesche**.*

Oh, it's not for me...I'm buying a **present** for my girlfriend.
*Oh, non è per me...compro un **regalo** per la mia ragazza.*

Briefs
I boxer briefs

Jock strap
Il sospensorio

Those boxers fit well.
Ti stanno bene i boxer.

Crazy for beautiful shoes
Una mania per le belle scarpe

Now, whether you like it or not, we all have a place on the ladder of life, and to the Italians, *le scarpe* (shoes) say more about where our notch is than any other article. If you're a shoe-hound, designer boots are a must-have. Watch out! Because Italy is about to make your bank account its bitch.

I like to wear....
Preferisco portare....
Literally, "I prefer to wear...."

Do you have **these**...in my size?
*Avete **queste**...nella mia misura?*

I totally have a **thing** for....
*Ho la **mania** per....*

> **tennis shoes**
> *le scarpe da tennis*
>
> **boots**
> *gli stivali*
>
> **heels**
> *i tacchi*

pumps
le scarpe scollate

high-heels
le scarpe con tacco alto
This term is used to describe the kind of heels that require you to avoid grass and mud at all costs.

lace-up shoes
le scarpe allacciate

pointed shoes
le scarpe a punta

sandals
i sandali

clogs
gli zoccoli
The masculine version of this noun means "clog," but the feminine *zoccola* is euphemistic for a prostitute. Don't mix them up!

stilettos
i tacchi a spillo

stockings
le calzatine

tights
i collants

fishnet stockings
le calze a rete

I like to go **barefoot**.
*Mi piace andare **scalzo/a**.*

What beautiful **ankles** you have!
*Che belle **caviglie** hai!*

I swear, she kept her **heels** on even in bed!
*Ti giuro, portava i **tacchi** anche a letto!*

Television
La televisione

There's no better way to *ammazzare il tempo* (kill time) than by watching Italian TV. On any given day, *fotomodelle* (models) with plumped lips and Botoxed foreheads share stories about their favorite *mutandine* (underwear). Newscasters that look like they just walked off the pages of *Vogue* discuss the *telegiornali* (news) of the day. Everyday folk sit in studio audiences and applaud on cue.

Reality shows like *Il Grande Fratello* (Big Brother) and *Isola dei Famosi* (Island of the Famous) are big hits in Italy. After all, there's no better way to feel good about yourself than to watch a bunch of desperate, attention-grabbing strangers quibble, squabble, and bicker while well-positioned cameras record every bloody *minuto.* And there's nothing like watching Caesar Milan on his show *The Dog Whisperer* (dubbed in Italian of course).

What do you wanna **watch**?
*Cosa vuoi **guardare**?*

What TV **shows** do you like?
*Che **programmi** ti piacciono?*

I was **channel surfing** when I came across some real artsy porn.
*Facevo **zapping** quando ho visto un film porno proprio artistico.*

What **channel** is that on?
*Su quale **canale** gira quel programma?*

Just so you know, the **remote** stays in my possession.
*Per la tua informazione, il **telecomando** rimane in mio possesso.*

Do you **wanna fuck** or watch TV?
***Vuoi scopare** o guardare la TV?*
Note that TV is pronounced tee-voo.

COOKING SHOWS
PROGRAMMI DI CUCINA

The best part of Italian television are the *programmi di cucina* (cooking shows) like *La Prova di Abilità* (*The Ability Challenge*), where winners get a chance to dine with their favorite singers, or *Stelle e Padelle* (*Stars and Pans*), where game contestants fight for the chance to open their own *ristorante* or have their *ricette* published in a book. *Il Mondo di un Bicchiere* (*The World of the Glass*) discusses everything involving drinks, mostly *il vino*, of course. *Pizza Passione* is a no-brainer. *Con i Piedi per Terra* (*With Feet on the Ground*) talks about Italian agriculture, the Slow Food Movement, and visiting Italy's many regions, all each with their own special *cucina*. And finally, imported directly from the States, *Top Chef* is watched by millions of Italians every week, many of whom are probably not eating anything nearly as good as what they're seeing prepared.

The movies
Il cinema

The Italians became obsessed with cinema almost as soon as the first projectors started making their way down to Italy from France back at the turn of the twentieth century. In those days, there were no vats of popcorn or gallons of soda; people watched from their terraces and the town's *piazza* as *lo spettacolo* was projected onto the sides of the medieval and ancient buildings (watch the Italian movie *Cinema Paradiso* to get an idea). The first major silent picture, *Cabiria*, by Giovanni Pastrone, came out in 1914, and it was notably one of the most important milestones in cinematic history. The impact those early flicks had on the Italian psyche has never left them.

Let's see a **movie**.
*Andiamo a vedere un **film**.*

What are the **show times?**
*Quale sono gli **orari dei film**?*

How long is it?
Quanto dura?

I prefer to watch movies on the **big screen.**
*Preferisco guardare i film sul **grande schermo.***

What **kinds** of movies do you like?
*Che **tipi** di film ti piacciono?*

I'm into....
Mi va....

action
azione

animation
animazione

adventure
avventura

biography
biografico

comedy
commedia

documentary
documentario

drama
drammatico

erotic
erotico

horror
horror

independent
indipendente

musical
musicale

pulp
giallo
"Yellow" films got their name from the fact that schmaltzy paperback crime novels and mysteries were typically identified by yellow covers.

science fiction
fantascienza

skin flicks
film blu
Literally, "blue films." Books considered risqué were identified by their blue covers when the printing of paperbacks made books much more accessible to the general population.

Communications
Le comunicazioni

These days, staying in touch (and getting some action) has never been easier. Millions of Italians surf the web, chat, blog, and text 24/7. Making a date is as simple as flipping open your *telefonino.* In addition to meeting new people through existing friends, the Italians regularly use the *annunci* (personal ads).

Italy is definitely online, but it's not as user friendly as, say, a super-techy destination like Toyko. The best thing to do before traveling is to have your phone unlocked and buy a local SIM card. This will facilitate usage of your phone map apps and ensure you can keep the lines open with *amici* and *famiglia* back home. TIM and Vodaphone are two major carriers and are usually located at the airport and in town. Or, if you are on Facebook Messenger, Viber, or Whatsapp, you can easily stay connected with family and friends back home. Many hotels claim to have high-speed, but often it's just a modem lodged in the back of an office. In that case, you might find better service in the lobby than your room.

Is there an **internet café** nearby?
*C'è un **café con internet** qui vicino?*

Internet cafés are a bit obsolete, as most coffee shops in major cities offer access, but along the beaten track, it might be more difficult to find access outside your hotel.

Do you have free Wi-Fi?
Avete Wi-Fi libero?

Where can I...?
Dove posso...?

> **check** my e-mail
> ***controllare** la mia posta elettronica*
> Italians also use the English word "e-mail."
>
> **download** a file
> ***scaricare** un file*
> Italians also like to use their version of the English, *daunlodare.*
>
> **browse** the web
> ***navigare** nella rete*
> Italians also use the term *surfare*, as in "surf the net."

What's your **e-mail address**?
*Qual è il tuo **indirizzo e-mail**?*

E-MAIL
E-MAIL

In Italian, the "at" (@) symbol used in e-mail addresses is called *chiocciola* ("snail"). The "dot" is *punto* ("period").

My e-mail address is [______] at [______] dot com.
Il mio indirizzo e-mail è [______] chiocciola [______] punto com.

To express "www." Italians say "*vuvuvu punto.*"

What **site** was that?
*Che **sito** era quello?*

Send me a **picture**.
*Invia una **foto** a me.*

Send me the link please.
***Mandami** il link per favore.*

Don't forget to **back up** the files.
*Non dimenticare di **backuppare** i file.*

Do you like to **chat** on the internet?
*Ti piace **ciattare** in rete?*

What's your **user name**?
*Qual è il tuo **nome utente**?*

Do I need a password?
Mi serve una password?
Also used is *parola d'ordine* and *la parola d'accesso.*

It costs less to **Skype** than to use a phone.
*Costa di meno **Skypare** che telefonare.*

To google
Googlare

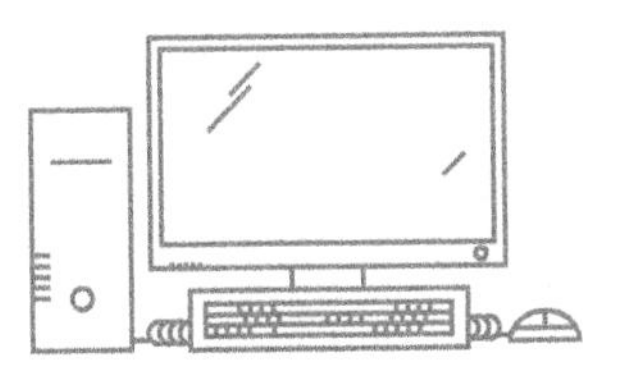

To use the internet
Internettare

To LOL
Lollare
This is an Italianization of the acronym LOL

To take a selfie
Selfare

Really good Twitter posts
Twitteratura
From "Twitter" + *letteratura*, meaning literature.

The telephone
Il telefono

Sit anywhere long enough and you'll hear someone's *telefonino* (aka *cellulare*) beep, sing, and vibrate.

ITALIAN ABBREVIATIONS
ABBREVIAZIONI ITALIANE

Texting is a language unto itself. If you're chatting online or someone sends you a text, you can consult this handy little glossary to understand what they've just said.

fdv	Felice di vederti.	Nice to see you.
risp	Rispondimi.	Answer me.
d6	Dove sei?	Where are you?
xfv	Per favore.	Please.
midi	Mi dispiace.	I'm sorry.
rds	Ride da solo.	LOL.
fct	Fatti i cazzi tuoi.	Mind your own fuckin' business.
ttp	Torno fra poco.	BRB.
ap	A presto.	C U soon.
sdr	Sogni d'oro.	Sweet dreams.
to	Ti odio.	I hate you.
hobidite	Ho bisogno di te.	I need you.
ta	Ti amo.	I love you.
mmt+	Mi manchi tantissimo.	I miss you so much.
tipe	Ti penso.	I'm thinking of you.
ba	Bacio.	Kiss.
xxx	Tanti baci.	A bunch of kisses.
ba&ab	Baci e abbracci.	Kiss and hugs.
abecba	Abbracciami, *eccitami, baciami.*	Hug me, excite me, kiss me.
tm	Tesoro mio.	My treasure.
am	Amore.	Love.
aminfi	Amore infinito.	Infinite love.
6 la +	Sei la migliore.	You're the best.
610	Sei uno zero.	You're a loser.
amxse	Amore per sempre.	Love forever.

What's your **number**?
*Qual è il tuo **numero di telefono**?*

I'll give you a **ring**.
*Ti faccio uno **squillo**.*

Can I **call** you?
*Ti posso **telefonare**?*

Hi, it's me.
Ciao, sono io.

Hello!
Pronto!
Italians answer the *telefono* with *Pronto!* ("Ready!") It goes back to the days when a switch operator needed to get everyone on the line before they were connected.

Fantastic! Is Peter there?
Fantastico! C'è Pietro?

I can't find my **charger**.
*Non posso trovare il **caricatore** del telefono.*

Gestures
I gesti

Due to the fact that many people still speak local dialects, some of which are largely incomprehensible to people from other parts of the country, Italians are notorious for their expressive body language and gestures. These ought to get you started.

Enough!
Basta!
Rub your hands together as if you were washing them.

Wonderful!
Bellissimo!
Kiss you fingertips.

Hey wise guy. Pay attention!

Che furbo. Attenzione!

Point your index finger to below your eye, and gently pull the bottom lid.

What shit luck!

Che sfiga!

Grab your family jewels and raise your eyebrows.

What balls./How boring.

Che palle.

Make an inverted L with the thumb and index fingers of both hands. With your index fingers pointing down, shake your hands up and down.

Delicious!

Delizioso!

Place your index finger on the corner of your mouth and turn it back and forth.

I'm hungry.

Ho fame.

Take your open-palmed hand and jab it into the side of your hip.

Oh, brother.

Madonna mia.

Bring your hands together as if you were praying, and tilt them up and down.

I could give a damn.

Me ne frego.

Flick your fingers outward from your chin while slightly tilting your chin.

Up yours!

Vaffanculo!

Place one hand inside the elbow of the opposite arm. Snap the opposite arm up with your hand open. I'm sure you're already familiar with this one...

No can do. I'm sorry.

Mi dispiace.

Make an L with your thumb and index finger (of both hands). Keeping the L formed, turn your thumbs outward and back several times.

I'll kick your ass!

Ti faccio un culo così!

Take both hands and form a circle with your index fingers and thumbs. Shake up and down.

Schmuck.

Cornuto.

Here you are imitating horns. Touch your middle and ring fingers to your thumb leaving your index and pinky fingers out like a tiny pair of horns. Lock your thumb around your tucked middle fingers. To express "knock on wood," make the same sign and point downward.

CHAPTER 8

Sports & Games

Lo Sport & Il Divertimento

La domenica (on Sundays), there's the church, and then there's soccer. If the local team wins and you're in a major *città* (city), don't be surprised to find yourself stuck in traffic while Italians blow their *clacson* (horns), wave their arms, and scream like hell. Modern Italians are an active bunch, and besides soccer, you'll find them at the *palestra* (gym) working out, playing tennis, or throwing around some cards. And of course, ever since the chariot games, spectators around the world can thank the Italians for combining speed with class (think Maserati, Ferrari, Ducati), not to mention the world-class bicycle race Giro d'Italia. Italians stay current by reading *La Gazzetta dello Sport*, a newspaper completely *dedicato* to sports.

Sports

Gli sport

What sports do you like?
Che sport preferisci?

Why don't we go **play**...?
*Perché non andiamo a **giocare**...?*

I do....
Faccio....

I play....
Io gioco....

Let's watch **some....**
Guardiamo ***un po'*** *di....*

auto racing
l'automobilismo

baseball
il baseball

basketball
la pallacanestro
The Americanized *il basket* is also used.

cycling
il ciclismo

dancing
la danza

football
il futball americano

golf
il golf

hockey
l'hockey

inline skating
il pattinaggio inline

jogging
il footing

MMA (Mixed Martial Arts)
MMA (pronounced emme emme ah) (Arti Marziali Miste)

ping-pong
il ping pong
Il tennis tavolo (table tennis) is also used.

racing
la corsa

soccer
il calcio
Literally, "the kick"; *il futball* is also used.

skateboarding
il monopattino

swimming
il nuoto

tennis
il tennis

weightlifting
il sollevamento pesi

weight training
i pesi
Short for *la pesistica.*

wrestling
la lotta libera; wrestling

yoga
lo yoga

Soccer
Il calcio

Veni, vidi, vici (I came, I saw, I conquered). Whether talking about sex or sports, this notorious Roman quotation still applies to Italy's national pastime. It's no understatement to say that Italians take their games *molto* seriously.

It's not hard to imagine that yesterday's *gladiatori* (gladiators) are today's *calciatori* (soccer players). The French, Spanish, and Brazilians may wince, but it's true—the Italian team is indisputably one of the best (and most beautiful) in the *mondo*. If you think the Super Bowl is a big deal, wait until you see *milioni* of Italians leaving work early in order to watch *i Mondiali* (the World Cup). When Italy plays, it's essentially a national *festa* (holiday).

Let's go to the **game**.
Andiamo alla ***partita****.*

What's your favorite **team**?
Qual è la tua ***squadra*** *preferita?*

The **crowd** was nuts.
La ***folla*** *era pazzesca.*

For the **fans**, soccer is practically a religion.
Per i ***tifosi****, il calcio è praticamente una religione.*

I'd like to buy a **game card**.
Vorrei comprare una ***schedina****.*
Equivalent to a lottery ticket.

It should be quite a **championship** this weekend.
Dovrà essere un ***campionato*** *strafigo questo weekend.*

Soccer players are like gods in Italy.
I calciatori *in Italia sono come gli dei.*

A challenge
Una sfida

A free kick
Un calcio di punizione

A head butt
Una testata

A pass
Un lancio

A penalty kick
Un calcio di rigore

A player
Il giocatore

A shot
Il tiro

A tie game
Un pareggio

Winning/losing games
Vinte/perse

The ball
Il pallone; La palla; La sfera
La sfera literally means "the sphere."

The coach
L'allenatore

The defender
Il difensore

The forward
L'attaccante

The goalie
Il portiere

The mass (of spectators)
La massa

The mob
La turba

The ref
L'arbitro

The soccer field
Il campo di calcio

The stadium
Lo stadio

The sweeper
Il libero

Way to go!

Forza!

If you really want to be like an Italian, join the *tifosi* (fans) and sing for your favorite team, or curse the competition. You should know that the two main *serie* (series) are A and B. This is where the top Italian teams compete. A lot of the players from Series A end up on the national team. Playing the numbers is big business, and everyone has a favorite team. For example, the Laziali are fans of the Lazio football club, while the *Rossoblu* (red and blue) are loyal to Bologna. In Milan, you'll hear the rants and raves of the *Rossoneri* (red and black), while the *Bianconeri* (white and black) are devotees of Juventus—you get the picture.

Italy's National Soccer team is called *gli Azzurri* ("The Azures") from "Azzurro Savoia" (Savoy Blue) and their blue shirts make it pretty easy to identify them. Try screaming some of the following cheers to egg on your *squadra* (team).

Come on!
Dai!

Go for it!
Evvai!

Nice goal!
Bel goal!

Here we go.
Ora ci siamo.

What a sexy move!
Che orgasmo!
Literally, "What an orgasm!"

Well done!
Bravo!

Hot damn, **what a game!**
Ammazza ***che partita!***

Kick the ball!
__Tira__ la palla!

Come on...score a goal already!
__Ma dai__...segna un goal!

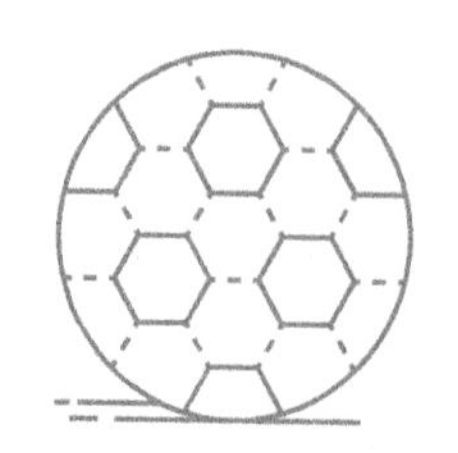

Crazy for kicks
Matto per il calcio

Slam, sneer, and snub the opposition using these multipurpose invectives. Smear some paint on your face, throw your arm up with your hand clenched in a fist, and yell as loud as you want, "*BASTARDO FIGLIO DI PUTTANA TESTA DI MERDA VAFFANCULO!*" Let it all out, *bambino mio*. For every goddam little thing that you've been keeping tucked deep inside you, now is the time to release. Here, you get to use your outside voice. Holla!

Your team **sucks**!
La vostra squadra __fa schifo__!

The ref is a turd.
__L'arbitro__ è uno stronzo.

Hey ref, you're a **schmuck**!
Arbitro __cornuto__!

He **fucked** up.
Ha fatto una __cazzata.__

What a **dud**!
Che __schiappa__!

Scram if you don't want more from where that came!
__Filate__ se non volete prenderne ancora.

Here comes **trouble.**
Arrivano i __guai__.

We've had it with this game.
__Ci siamo rotti__ con questa partita.

What a **shitty game.**
Che ***partita di merda.***

This game **sucked.**
Questa partita è stata ***uno schifo.***

He was kicked off the team for swearing.
È stato espulso *dalla squadra per bestemmie.*

The Italian team **whooped** the French team.
La squadra Italiana ***ha fatto polpetta*** *della squadra Francese.*
Literally, "made meatballs out of."

The French took **a beating** from the Italians—as usual.
I Francesi sono stati ***massacrati*** *dagli Italiani—come sempre.*

Working out
Fare la ginnastica

There are plenty of places to get your blood pumping in Italy—you've got your *palestra* (gym), your cycling courses, and your *muro per arrampicata* (rock-climbing wall). Lots of Italians are hippied out now and regularly do yoga, karate, Pilates, *lo spinning* (spinning), and *meditazione* (meditation).

Let's go to **the gym.**
Andiamo in ***palestra.***

Want to **go lift**?
Vuoi andare a ***farti quattro pesi****?*

Can you **spot me**?
Puoi ***controllarmi****?*

Exercise helps reduce my **cellulite.**
La ginnastica aiuta a diminuire la ***cellulite.***

He's/She's totally....
È completamente....

GIDDYUP HORSIE: THE PALIO
ANDIAMO A CAVALLO: IL PALIO

Since the thirteenth century, the Palio in Siena has enjoyed a reputation for being one of the most unpredictable *corsa da cavalli* (horse races) in the world. Winning is everything, and it doesn't matter what methods you use. It's like capitalism for sports: Playing dirty, fixing races, and cutting bribes are all par for the course.

The race takes place in Siena's central Piazza del Campo, where loads of dirt are trucked in to form the track. Every July and August, over 50,000 *spettatori* (spectators) come to watch the races, which begin with huge *processioni* (processions) of trumpet players, drummers, and flag bearers representing the colors of their *contrada* (district).

Only ten *contrade* are chosen by lottery to participate in a given race. The horses are also drawn by lottery and assigned to the participating districts, preventing (theoretically) any attempts to disable a prized steed. *I fantini* (jockeys) aren't even essential to win. If a horse arrives at the finish line without its jockey, its *contrada* still wins.

If you visit Siena during the races, don't let anything keep you from screaming for your favorite *contrada* and calling the competitors' sisters a bunch of *puttane* (whores).

Go back to your mommy!
***Torna** dalla mamma!*

Your **jockey** is a little turd!
*Il vostro **fantino** è uno stronzetto!*

cut
definito/a

huge
enorme

ripped
muscoloso/a

sculpted
scolpito/a

toned
tonico/a

I want to work out my....
Voglio concentrarmi su....

abs
gli addominali

arms
le braccia

ass
il culo

back
la schiena

biceps
i bicipidi

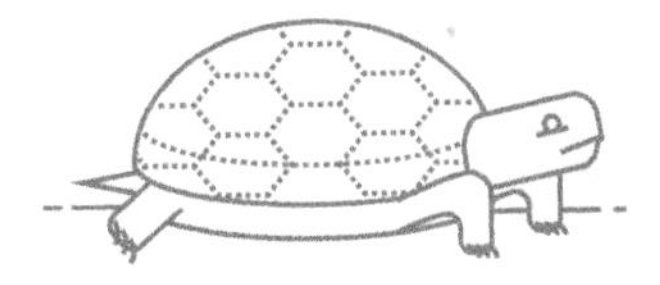

glutes
i glutei

legs
le gambe

pecs
i pettorali

triceps
i tricipidi

Check out my **six-pack.**
Guarda la ***tartaruga.***
Literally, "turtle." Kinda reminds you of the Ninja Turtles, no?

Do you know where I can find a good **dance studio**?
Sai dove posso trovare uno ***studio di danza****?*

For every diet, you gotta **burn the fat.**
Per un programma dimagrante è necessario ***bruciare i grassi.***

How do you **stay in shape** without going to the gym?
Come ***rimani in forma*** *senza andare in palestra?*

How do Italians manage to eat so well and still have **lean legs** and **flat stomachs**?
*Come fanno gli Italiani a mangiare bene ed anche ad avere le **gambe snelle** e gli **addominali piatti**?*

Games
I giochi

The Italian expression *il dolce far niente* essentially translates to "the sweetness of doing nothing"—in other words, hanging out. *Il dolce far niente* implies a certain connoisseurship for relaxation. Especially now that the world economy has turned to shit, if there's ever a place to enjoy the here and now, it's Italy. There will always be difficult times, but with a good bottle of wine and the right company, it's not so bad.

Backgammon
La tavola reale

Pool
I biliardi

Checkers
La dama

Playing cards
Le carte da gioco
Italians have been playing cards since the 1500s. Popular games include Bestia, Briscola, Scopa, Sette e Mezzo (Seven and a Half), and Tressette (Three Sevens). Scopa is a very popular game with cards that resemble the tarot. This word is not to be confused with *una scopata*, which means "a fuck."

Poker
Il poker

Video games
I giochi video

Italians aren't exactly known for being gamers like you see in the U.S. and Japan. A lot of young Italians hit the *sala di giochi* (arcade), although these days, most Italians are getting their fix with *giochi online* (online games).

Do you have a...?
Avete...?

PlayStation
Playstation

Xbox
X-Box

Nintendo
Nintendo

Wii
Wii

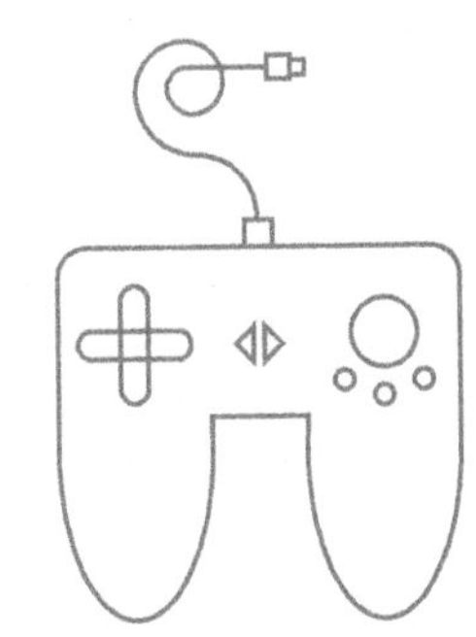

Yo, pass the **controller**.
*Dai, passami il **comando**.*

Use the **trigger** to kill those little green things.
*Schiaccia il **grilletto** per ammazzare quelle cosine verdi.*

Why would Princess ever date Mario? He's a short, little, chubby dude with a '70s porn mustache.
Ma perchè mai la Principessa uscirebbe con Mario? È un tappo chiatto con i baffi stile pornostar degli anni Settanta.

Yeah, but he's a total hipster!
Sì, ma lui è proprio un uomo hipster!

CHAPTER 9

Dining & Desserts

Il Mangiare

Italians live to eat. They spend more time on meals—shopping, preparing, and cleaning up after them—than anything else. Is it any surprise that Italians even have *gelato per i cani* (ice cream for dogs)? For the *prima colazione* (breakfast), most Italians eat a *brioche* with a *cappuccino* or *latte macchiato*. Thanks to Starfucks, you should be familiar with these common Italian beverages.

Il pranzo (lunch) is another story. You'll be hard-pressed to find a soul who works through the midday break, which usually consists of *un piatto* (a plate) of pasta or a bowl of soup and a glass of wine. *La cena* (dinner) is eaten later in Italy. Most *ristoranti* (restaurants) aren't even open before 7:00 p.m., and that's still considered on the early side.

Hunger

La fame

Italians use the word *affamato* to say "hungry"; *la fame* describes "hunger," whether it's the kind involving your stomach or the type that has to do with your second chakra (that's the groin region, FYI).

Are you **hungry**?
*Hai **fame**?*

I'm **sooooo** hungry.
*Ho **tantissima** fame.*

I could eat a horse.
Sono proprio allupato/a.
Allupato can mean "hungry" as well as "horny" and comes from the word *lupo* (wolf), an animal given a lot of clout in Italy. For example, you'll also find the wolf in the phrase *Ho una fame da lupo* ("I'm hungry as a wolf"). Every guidebook will remind you of the fact that Romulus (who founded Rome) and his twin, Remus, were suckled by a she-wolf.

I could die from hunger!
***Potrei morire** dalla fame!*

I'm dying of thirst!
***Sto morendo** di sete!*

I'm friggin' starving!
Ho una fame da morti!
Literally, "I have a hunger of the dead." *Da morti* can be used as a superlative with many things to say "very." For example, *Ho un sonno da morti* ("I'm dead tired").

Have you **already** eaten?
*Hai **già** mangiato?*

Let's eat!
Mangiamo!

It's chow time!
A tavola!
Literally, "to the table."

I'm in the mood for...
Mi va...

What are you in the mood for?
Cosa ti va?
Va, the imperative form of the verb *andare* (to go), is used in many idiomatic expressions such as *Vattene!* (Get outta here!) and *Vaffanculo!* (Up yours!)

Thanks, but I'm on a diet.
*Grazie, ma sono a **dieta**.*

Why don't we have a **drink**?
*Perché non ci facciamo una **bevutina**?*

Yummy!
Squisito!

Everybody in Italy knows how to sing the "Ave Maria," but it's equally important to sing praises to the chef.

Compliments to the chef!
***Complimenti** al cuoco!*

Delicious!
Delizioso!

Incredible!
Incredibile!

Taste it!
Assaggialo!

You've gotta try this!
Dai, prova questo!

Outta this world!
Fuori mondo!

This dish is like an **orgasm in my mouth**.
*Questo piatto è come un **orgasmo nella bocca**.*

This pizza is **really good.**
*Questa pizza è **buonissima**.*

Scrumptious!
Squisito!

Yummy!
Che buono!

I ate like a **whale.**
*Ho mangiato come una **balena**.*

I stuffed myself like a pig.
***Mi sono abbuffato** come un maiale.*

I'm full.
Sono pieno/a.

Excuse me!
Mi scusi!

Snapping your fingers and yelling is far less effective than a respectable *Mi scusi* when trying to get the attention of your *cameriere* (waiter). And when the time comes to settle up, remember that most Italian establishments don't bring *il conto* (the bill) until you ask for it, and even then, they'll take their time. Also, remember that it's best to call the waiter *Signore* or *Signora.*

Can I have...?
Posso avere...?

> **the menu**
> *la lista*
>
> **a fork**
> *una forchetta*
>
> **a knife**
> *un coltello*
>
> **a spoon**
> *un cucchiaio*
>
> **a napkin**
> *un tovagliolo*

What **are we eating**?
*Cosa **mangiamo**?*

Excuse me, we'd like **to order**, thanks.
*Mi scusi, vorremo **ordinare**, grazie.*

We're in a **rush.**
Abbiamo ***fretta.***

I could eat you for **dinner**.
Potrei mangiarti per la ***cena****.*

What are you doing later on?
Che cosa fai *più tardi?*
If your waiter or waitress is cute, why not give it a shot?

What do you **recommend**?
Che cosa ***raccomanda****?*

What's in this **dish**?
Di che cosa consiste questo ***piatto****?*

Can you bring the **check**, please.
Ci porti il ***conto****, per favore.*

This one's on me.
Offro io.

Should we leave a **tip**?
Lasciamo una ***mancia****?*
Leaving *una mancia* is optional, since you're paying *il coperto* (a cover charge) for both the service and the *pane*, but it's cool to leave a little extra something.

How gross!
Che schifo!

Uttered by millions every day, *Che schifo!* literally translates to "How gross!" The noun *uno schifo* refers to "a gross thing" and can be easily changed to the adjective *schifoso* (gross, or disgusting). The verbiage *fare schifo* is used to indicate something or someone of inferior quality, as in "it sucks."

This pizza **sucks**!
Questa pizza ***fa schifo****!*

That was **awful**!
Era ***pessimo****!*

That meal was **crap**.
Quel pasto era di ***merda***.

That restaurant has the **worst service.**
Quel ristorante ha un ***servizio proprio sgarbato***.

That restaurant **sucked.**
Il ristorante era uno ***schifo***.

The idea of eating horsemeat **turns my stomach**.
L'idea di mangiare la carne di cavallo ***mi dà allo stomaco***.

A dog wouldn't eat this.
Non lo mangerebbe neanche un cane.

I found a **hair** in my pasta.
Ho trovato un ***capello*** *nella pasta.*

This is so bland.
Questo non ha né amore né sapore.
Literally, "This has neither love nor taste." Notice the rhyme.

This has a **nasty taste**.
Questo ha un ***sapore cattivo***.

This'll make you **vomit**.
Questo è da ***vomitare.***

Too many cooks **spoil** the broth.
Troppi cuochi ***guastano*** *la cucina.*

Pasta puttanesca?

Pasta puttanesca?

It's time to have a *spaghettata! Spaghettata* is a slang word that describes a meal that is spontaneously thrown together for a group of friends. All you need is a *bottiglia di vino* (bottle of wine) served alongside a steaming bowl of home-cooked *pasta puttanesca*.

Originating in Napoli, *pasta puttanesca* (literally, "whore pasta") got its name from the local prostitutes—the *puttane*—because it was fast, cheap, and spicy. Not to mention yummy. For those of you who are all thumbs in the kitchen, it's hard to mess this one up.

1 small onion, chopped	*una cipolla, tritata*
a little olive oil	*un po' d'olio d'oliva*
2 cloves of garlic	*2 spicchi d'aglio*
4 anchovies, chopped	*4 acciughe, tritate*
2 chile peppers	*2 peperoncini*
a handful of capers	*dei capperi*
a handful of black olives	*delle olive*
a small can of tomato sauce	*un piccolo contenitore di pomodori pelati*
a pinch of salt	*un pizzico di sale*
a pinch of black pepper	*un pizzico di pepe*
Italian parsley, chopped	*il prezzemolo, tritato*
a box of spaghetti	*una scatola di spaghetti*

In a saucepan, cook the onion in the olive oil on medium-high heat until it begins to caramelize. Add the garlic and anchovies and cook for a minute. Add the remaining ingredients except the spaghetti and the parsley, and bring to a boil.

Reduce the heat and simmer uncovered for 10 minutes, stirring occasionally.

While the sauce is simmering, cook the pasta. Make sure you don't overcook it; Italians eat their pasta *al dente* (literally, "to the tooth"), chewy like steak. Drain the cooked pasta. Gently stir the pasta and sauce together and sprinkle with chopped parsley.

Starters, sides, & soups

Gli antipasti e i contorni

Porcini mushrooms

Funghi porcini

Plump and meaty mushrooms that look like little pigs.

"Big stink"

Puzzone

A particularly fragrant cheese.

Sopa caôda

Sopa caôda

A Venetian soup consisting of pigeon and cabbage.

"Piss in the bed" soup

Zuppa di piscialetto

Italians don't mince words; made from dandelions, this soup is known for its diuretic effect.

First courses

I primi & i sughi

Fried omelette

Frittata

When you say *Che frittata!* it means a real mess.

Devil-style pasta

Pasta alla diavola

Pasta with a spicy tomato sauce.

Ladies' curls

Ricci di donna

A very curly type of pasta.

"Strangle the priest" pasta

Strozzapreti/strangolapreti

A hand-rolled noodle that resembles the rope once used to hang criminals and other deviants.

Main courses
I secondi

Cured pork rump
Culatello
Literally, "big ass."

Turkey cock
Gallinaccio
Yup.

The virtues
Le virtù
A dish involving seven ingredients representing seven virgins. In myth it was claimed to be a powerful aphrodisiac.

Chubby monk
Monacone
With its layers of eggplant, veal, prosciutto, tomato, and fontina, this dish has enough calories to last a winter, hence the name.

Horse stew
Pastissada di cavallo
A stew made from horsemeat and served with polenta.

Devil-style chicken
Pollo alla diavola
Chicken that is seasoned with chile peppers or black pepper.

The fifth quarter
Quinto quarto
This refers to the organs, brains, hooves, and testicles of a butchered animal.

Monkfish
Rana pescatrice
This guy is one ugly friggin' fish.

Grilled lamb guts
Stighiole

A popular Sicilian street food.

Saltimbocca
Saltimbocca
Literally, "jump in the mouth," this Roman specialty consists of veal, prosciutto, and sage, sautéed in butter.

Tripe
Trippa
Eating tripe is like eating rubber bands drenched in tomato sauce.

Stewed spleen sandwich
Vastedda
A Sicilian treat.

Carnival of delights
Il carnevale dei delitti

Italian cuisine is as diverse as the country itself. You name it, and there's a dish for it. Many foods are known *afrodisiaci* (aphrodisiacs), which appeal to the five senses and are designed to arouse and titillate. Here are a few of the more commonly known aphrodisiacs.

Almonds
Le mandorle
Almond *confetti* (confections) are given at weddings to represent both the bitter and sweet sides of marriage. They encourage a fertile and fruitful coupling, and their shape is reminiscent of the female genitalia. Popular desserts such as Cantucci, Amaretti, and Torrone all call for almonds.

Anise
L'anice
During the Middle Ages, *l'anice* was believed to increase arousal and help soften up young (and probably terrified) young brides. It is the main ingredient used in Sambuca and other recipes.

Artichokes
I carciofi

In 77 AD, the Roman historian Pliny the Elder mentions *i carciofi* in his book *Naturalis Historia*, and the Queen of the Renaissance, Caterina Di Medici, also used them in her kitchens. Believed to stimulate the libido, the notion of using one's fingers to peel away the outer leaves until reaching to the heart also symbolized undressing.

Basil

Il basilico

Basil, the main ingredient in pesto, is mentioned in Boccaccio's Decameron and is known as the "love herb" because it supposedly encourages *la passione*.

Chocolate

La Cioccolata

Lovers know that Italian chocolates are among the finest in the world. The Piedmont region is famous for its *giandujotti o gianduiotti* confections, which are made with hazelnuts. Sicily is renowned for its *granular cioccolato modicano*, a recipe that goes back to the fifteenth century. If you can, visit Perugia, Italy's chocolate capital.

Figs

I Fichi

Figs are a very symbolic and delicious aphrodisiac. It's no wonder the word in singular form has come to mean a hottie while also referring to the female genitalia.

Garlic

L'aglio

Garlic is a much appreciated aphrodisiac probably for the fact that it's so good for you.

Hot peppers

I peperoncini

The hot pepper you see worn by Italian men ain't just an ordinary veggie. Representing the horn, and also the male sex, hot peppers are great for getting the blood flowing and are used in a number of recipes to enhance the love experience.

Truffles

I tartufi

Truffles are a known aphrodisiac because of their elusive nature and intrinsic medicinal qualities. Their musky scent stimulates the skin and they actually contain androstenol, a pheromone found in men's underarm sweat.

Salami
I Salumi
Yes, some women claim that eating salami makes them want to have sex, which of course makes all those salami shops a great place to pick up hungry women.

Sweets
I dolci

Italians are known for their sweets, including *gelato, panna cotta* (cooked cream), *granite, cannoli, affogato,* and *semifreddo*, but there are quite a few that deserve particular mention due to their colorful names.

Candied nuts
Addormenta suocere
Candied nuts that supposedly send mothers-in-law off into a deep sleep.

Dead men's beans
Fave dei morti
Fava bean–shaped cookies eaten on All Soul's Day, November 2.

Cat tongues
Lingue di gatto
Thin butter cookies.

St. Agatha's nipples
Minne di Sant'Agata
Breast-shaped cookies honoring the martyr St. Agatha.

Dead men's bones
Ossi di morti
A cookie molded in the shape of a shank bone. The name is somewhat redundant, but you get the picture.

Passion bread
Panettone della passione
A cakelike bread from Florence that's supposed to ignite the flames of love.

Tiramisu
Tiramisù
Made from espresso, ladyfingers, and mascarpone, along with a dash of rum. With the literal translation of "pick-me-up," you'll be flying in no time.

Three flies
Tre mosche
Refers to the coffee beans occasionally dropped into Sambuca that look like—you guessed it—flies.

Holy wine
Vin santo
A sweet wine, super high in alcohol, likely to bring anyone to a near ecstatic state; usually consumed during dessert.

Eat like an Italian

Mangiare come un Italiano

Even if you consider yourself a veteran eater of *la cucina italiana* (Italian cuisine), there are a few things you might want to keep in mind the next time you dine in Italy. Try to stay open-minded.

- **Don't ask for a doggy bag.** Italians never take doggie bags from a *ristorante* unless they actually have one of the four-legged guys back home; it's very gauche.
- **Don't snack.** Italians don't snack much, saving their *appetito* for the main meals.
- **Eat lunch.** Italians used to sit down and have a meal that *mamma* or *nonna* had been cooking all day. Nowadays, Italians grab a bite at the local bar, which is more like a café than a pub. What makes their bars different is the fact that

they actually drink and eat, and there's more than germ-ridden popcorn offered.

- **Wait!** *Aspetta!* When it comes to *le feste* (holidays) like *Natale* (Christmas) and *Pasqua* (Easter), try not to engulf everything you see, because more will be coming shortly. And *più e più* (more and more)...
- **Cheese, please.** Many Americans have had their minds blown upon discovering that Italians don't use gobs of melted *formaggio* (cheese) on every pasta dish served.
- **Espresso.** If you're drinking espresso in Italy, just ask for *un caffé*. *Cappuccino* is for breakfast and sometimes an afternoon pick-me-up, but never drunk after a meal. (Only *turisti* do that.) Also, don't expect a little slice of lemon rind on the edge of your cup—this is a primarily done in Italian-American communities.
- **Picking up the tab.** If you're going out for *caffé* with friends, it's typical that one person picks up the tab this time. The other gets it next time. You'll look like *un tirchio*—a real cheap turd—if you start pulling out coins from your pockets.
- **Sambuca.** Most Italians do not order *sambuca* (an anise-flavored liqueur) after every meal, nor do they throw coffee beans in the drink like is typically done in just about every Italian-American eatery with a checkered tablecloth. But do indulge in a *digestivo*.
- **Bread.** *Il burro* (butter) is never served with *pane* (bread) because it's expected that the bread will be *fresco* (fresh). *Il pane* is included with the cover charge.

Acknowledgments

I'd like to take a moment to thank all the people at Ulysses Press that have made this linguistic adventure possible. A big *grazie* to Shayna Keyles and Alice Riegert for their terrific editing of this book, and Damon Meibers at what!design for illustrations and design.

A special thanks to all the readers that have shared their insights and stories, and to you reading this now.

This book is a linguistic binge that is puerile, immature, unenlightened, and base. It's *merda*-talk, after all. But it's poetry too, with sweetly simple metaphors that, while not always pretty, remind us of what's *vero* (true). Plus, the therapeutic aspects of swearing are undeniable!

There's a long history of authors being banned because their words offended. Those are probably the same writers whose combustic humor makes you smile despite yourself. In homage to them, I submit the Italian *espressioni* and idioms within in order to assist the language learner in his or her *viaggio*.

About the Author

Gabrielle Euvino has an M.A. in international education from New York University and a B.A. in Italian language and literature from the State University of New York (College at New Paltz). Gabrielle is a translator and an adjunct professor of Italian and cross-cultural communications. She has written numerous books and articles about the Italian language including *The Complete Idiot's Guide to Learning Italian*, now in its fourth edition, and *The Pocket Idiot's Guide to Italian* (both by Alpha Books). More language-related material can be accessed on her Facebook page, La Bella Lingua Italiana. She is founder of Creative Language Arts and La Bella Lingua. She has been interviewed on Sirius Radio and profiled in newspaper and magazine articles.

Printed in the USA
CPSIA information can be obtained
at www.ICGtesting.com
CBHW072006040624
9537CB00010B/203